ESTRENO Collection of Contemporary Spanish Plays

General Editor: Martha T. Halsey

YOURS FOR THE ASKING

WITHDRAWN
UTSA LIBRARIES

WITHDRAWN
UTSA LIBRARIES

RECEIVED

APR 1 1 1995

UTSA Library Serials

ANA DIOSDADO

YOURS FOR THE ASKING

(Usted también podrá disfrutar de ella)

Translated by Patricia W. O'Connor

ESTRENO
Unversity Park, Pennsylvania
1995

ESTRENO Contemporary Spanish Plays 7
General Editor: Martha T. Halsey
                 Department of Spanish, Italian and Portuguese
                 College of the Liberal Arts
                 The Pennsylvania State University
                 University Park PA 16802 USA

Library of Congress Cataloging in Publication Data
Diosdado, Ana, 1938-
    Yours for the Asking
    Bibliography:
    Contents: Yours for the Asking
    Translation of: Usted también podrá disfrutar de ella
    1. Diosdado, Ana, 1938- Translation, English.
I. O'Connor, Patricia W. II. Title.
Library of Congress Catalog Card No.: 94-72547
ISBN: 0-9631212-6-X

© 1995 Copyright by ESTRENO

Original play © Ana Diosdado: Usted también podrá disfrutar de ella, 1974.

Translation © Patricia W. O'Connor 1995
First Edition
All rights reserved
No part of this publication may be reproduced or transmitted in any form or
by any means, electronic or mechanical, including photocopy, recording, or
any information storage or retrieval system now known or to be invented,
without permission in writing from the publishers, except by a reviewer who
wishes to quote brief passages in connection with a review written for
inclusion in a magazine, newspaper, or broadcast.

The publishers wish to acknowledge with thanks
financial assistance for the translation from the
Dirección General del Libro y Bibliotecas
of the Ministerio de Cultura de España.

Published with Support from
The Program of Cultural Cooperation Between
Spain's Ministry of Culture and the United States Universities

Cover: Jeffrey Eads

Library
University of Texas
at San Antonio

A NOTE ON THE PLAY

What is remarkable about this 1973 Spanish play is its uncanny timeliness in 1994 America. It evokes the power of the press to invent celebrities and destroy them, journalists who pander to a sensation-seeking readership, the shallowness of relationships in a society that prizes physical attractiveness and success, a mass audience that cannot distinguish between media-created creatures and reality, the intolerance of the "man in the street" whose emotions have been manipulated by advertising, and the unaccountability of some profit-making operations hidden deep within the corporate conglomerate.

One might expect a play incorporating such themes to be a lumbering, agenda-driver vehicle, but *Yours for the Asking* is essentially the story of a man and a woman whose potential for love and for making a positive contribution to their world are stymied partly by circumstances, but mostly by their own methods of grappling with life. Both sell themselves out, because they sell themselves short.

Juan, a 38-year-old journalist, takes a cynical view of life. Though his convictions earned him prison time during the Franco regime, he has no faith in the individual's power to make a difference. Suddenly given an opportunity to make a difference in the life of a lovely 20-year-old model, Juan must confront the hopelessness with which he has become almost comfortable. Susi is an innocent whose appearance in a TV commercial for a new perfume called "She" ("She" is... yours for the asking) leads to her being victimized by the media, by commercial interests, and even by ordinary people. Both Juan and Susi feel trapped and alone, a condition that finds brilliant theatrical reification when each is trapped in turn in an apartment-building elevator cage.

The theatricality of this socially-relevant, psychological comedy-drama is one of its strengths. The perfume advertisement that serves as a springboard for the action is presented as a visual prelude. Suspense builds steadily as clues accumulate throughout the skillfully deconstructed narrative and build it to a surprising yet somehow inevitable climax.

The introduction of the work of Ana Diosdado, Spain's foremost living woman playwright, to the American stage is long overdue. The provocative content and technical virtuosity of *Yours for the Asking* make it an excellent choice with which to begin seeing her plays.

Felicia Hardison Londré
Dramaturg Missouri Repertory Theatre

ABOUT THE PLAYWRIGHT

Ana Diosdado was born in 1938 in Buenos Aires, the city to which her parents had emigrated to escape the ravages of the Spanish Civil War (1936-39). Her mother died when Ana was a baby, and she was reared by her father, Enrique Diosdado, Spain's premier actor, and his second wife, the similarly prestigious Amelia de la Torre. Given her role models, it is not surprising that Ana made her acting debut very early--at the age of six. She also wrote creatively very young, well before returning with her family to Spain in 1950.

Although Ana Diosdado has enjoyed considerable recognition as an actress and published her first novel in 1965, it is as a writer for stage and television that she is best known. Diosdado has found favor with Spain's audiences and critics since the performance of her first play, *Olvida los tambores* (1970; Forget the Drums). Acclaimed for her impeccable dramatic technique, she is the only woman whose work is represented in *Teatro español* (1949 to 1974), an annual anthology featuring the five major "hits" of each season. Included there are Diosdado's second and third plays, *El okapi* (1972; The Okapi) and *Usted también podrá disfrutar de ella* (1973; *Yours for the Asking*). Other well-known works include: *Los comuneros* (1974; The Cities Revolt), *Y de Cachemira, chales* (1976; And from Kashmere, Shawls), *Cuplé* (1986; Popular Song), *Los ochenta son nuestros* (1988; The Eighties Are Ours), *Camino de plata* (1989; Silvery Path), *Trescientos veintiuno, trescientos veintidós* (1991; Three Hundred Twenty One, Three Hundred Twenty Two) and *Cristal de Bohemia* (1994; Bohemian Crystal).

In addition to the original plays, Diosdado has adapted for stage Williams' *Cat on a Hot Tin Roof* (1979), Ibsen's *A Doll's House* (1983) and Wilde's *Lady Windemere's Fan* (1992) and continues active as novelist, short-story writer and journalist. She has also composed and directed two prize-winning television series in which she plays the leading role: "Anillos de oro" (Golden Wedding Rings, 1985) and "Segunda enseñanza" (Secondary Education, 1987). In preparation is "Yo, la juez" (I, the Judge), a television series in which Diosdado will play the title-role professional woman.

Ana Diosdado lives in Madrid with her actor husband, Carlos Larrañaga, who often performs in her plays and filmscripts and who also directed *Camino de plata*, a three-character work in which he, Ana and their daughter-in-law, Silvia Leblanc, performed.

ANA DIOSDADO

ABOUT THE TRANSLATOR

Patricia W. O'Connor, founder of the Spanish theater journal, *Estreno,* and editor from 1975 to 1992, is professor of Spanish at the University of Cincinnati where she received the Rieveschil Award for Scholary Work in 1983, holds the title "Distinguished Research Professor" and is a Fellow of the Graduate School. Her other published play translations include works by Antonio Buero Vallejo, Jaime Salom, Miguel Mihura, Carlos Muñiz, Lauro Olmo, Antonio Gala, Antonio Martínez Mediero, Alfonso Paso and Juan Antonio Castro. She has written numerous articles and several books on contemporary Spanish theater and in 1990 was elected Corresponding Member of Spain's Royal Academy of Language.

Usted también podrá disfrutar de ella was first staged at the Beatriz Theater in Madrid on November 28, 1973 under the direction of José Antonio Páramo.

CAUTION: Professionals and amateurs are hereby warned that *Yours for the Asking*, being fully protected under the Copyright Laws of the United States of America, the British Empire, including the Dominion of Canada, and all other countries covered by the Pan-American Copyright Convention and the Universal Copyright Conventions and of all countries with which the United States has reciprocal copyright relations, is subject to royalty. All rights, including professional, amateur, motion picture, recitation, public reading, radio and television broadcasting, and the rights of translation into foreign languages, are strictly reserved. Particular emphasis is laid on the question of readings, permission for which must be secured in writing.

Inquiries regarding permission should be addressed to the author through the
Sociedad General de Autores de España
Fernando VI, 4
28004 Madrid Spain

or to the author through the translator:
The Department of Romance Languages and Literatures
University of Cincinnati, OH 45221.

Act One of 1973 Madrid production at Beatriz Theater under direction of José Antonio Páramo. Fernando Guillén as Juan, María José Goyanes as Susi and Emilio Gutiérrez Caba as Manny. Photo by Gyenes.

CHARACTERS

Susi
Juan
Celia
Manny
The "Man in the Street" (Martinez, Coroner, Neighbor, Super, Agent, all played by the same actor)

Projected on the closed curtain is a huge billboard advertisement of a nude young woman being showered with rose petals. Splashed across the image is the product slogan:

SHE is. . . yours for the asking

The curtain opens slowly on a movie screen showing a TV commercial featuring the young woman of the billboard. She runs nude in slow motion on a bed of roses toward the camera. The background music can be by Bach, Corelli, Albinoni--any classical composer except Mozart. The image, softly diffused at first, becomes sharper as the young woman   approaches the camera. When very close, she gazes upward in ecstasy as the shower of rose petals continues.

AD VOICE-OVER: SHE is... yours for the asking. SHE... can make life wonderful, happy, full of promise... Come with us, and you will see. Come with us, and SHE... will fill your life with fragrance. SHE is... yours for the asking...

With the announcer's final words, superimposed on the screen image is:

SHE
a fragrance by York

The screen disappears, and the lights come up slowly as the action begins. The props and other staging elements should be kept to an absolute minimum; everything that can be suggested should be eliminated. Only words and attitudes are specified. The characters move in undefined places and times, and occasionally there is simultaneous action in different areas. The stage will be a space in which anything can happen.

ACT I

JUAN, thirty-eight years old, enters carrying a tape recorder. Looking tired and defeated, he goes over to the table and puts down the recorder. He picks up the telephone as though suddenly wanting to make a call but changes his mind. Finally, he sits down at a typewriter, puts a sheet of paper in the carriage, lights a cigarette and begins to type.

The telephone rings. JUAN grabs the phone expectantly.

JUAN: Yes? (*He sighs, disappointed but resigned, when he recognizes the caller's voice.*) Oh, hello. What's up?.... Sure, I just got in... With her, with the girl.... (*Speaking louder.*) I said with the girl!.... Yes, until today, until just now. (*Looking at his watch.*) Well, until half an hour ago, the time it took me to get here... Yes, mostly talking... Talking, I said! Why don't you put the phone on your other ear?... Yes, we spent the week talking... Sure I interviewed her. I was just beginning to write the article... (*Getting impatient.*) Of course I started to work as soon as I got in. I'm the model employee, wouldn't you say?... Yes, it's going to be wonderful. All your little housewives are going to swoon with ecstasy in the beauty parlors... Beauty parlors, I said! Isn't that where they read us?... No, that's not optimism; it's more like disgust. I just can't take it anymore.... Can't take it, I said!... Yes, tons of pictures... No, Manny took them. Julio had a photo session with a countess... Yes, lots of bare leg and all the closeups you could ask for. You're going to love it... I said Thursday, didn't I? That means it'll be on your desk in a few hours. Look, I'm in no mood to talk right now. See you later.

(He hangs up. Only then does he realize that there is someone else in the room, observing him. CELIA, in her pajamas, looks as though she has just gotten out of bed. Twenty-five or thirty years old and pretty, she treats JUAN affectionately, but with a hint of maternal over-protection. His tone suggests that he is distracted and thinking about something else.)

JUAN: What are you doing here?
CELIA: I live here, remember?
JUAN: What I meant was: what are you doing up at this hour?
CELIA (*Smiling as she looks at him*): Just taking in the view...
JUAN: You've seen it plenty of times before.
CELIA: You're right, and it's looking all parched and wilted at the moment. But I like it anyway.
JUAN: How nice.

CELIA: You're welcome.

JUAN: That doesn't follow.

CELIA: What doesn't?

JUAN: I said "How nice," not "Thank you."

CELIA (*Noticing something strange*): Are you all right?

JUAN: Yes.

CELIA: You don't look it. And it's four in the morning. Aren't you going to get some sleep?

JUAN: I can't. I have to write a wonderful article about this wonderful young model.

CELIA: Right now?

JUAN: Martinez wants the copy on his desk by nine.

CELIA (*Remembering*): Yes, he's been trying to reach you all week. He starts calling in the morning and keeps at it.

(*CELIA pauses for a moment to see if he will say something else, but he is absorbed in his papers. As CELIA observes him, she catches something imperceptible to anyone else. Friends and lovers, CELIA and JUAN know each other well. Their jokes, ironies and even their reproaches are simply different expressions of the bond common to people who live and work together. The principal difference between them is that CELIA is strong and JUAN is weak.*)

CELIA (*Attacking, but in a good-natured way*): How about some coffee?

JUAN: How about your going back to bed?

CELIA: How about your letting me plan my own schedule?

JUAN: And how about your not treating me like a child?

CELIA: Why don't you just tell me if you want some coffee?

JUAN: Why don't you come out with it?

CELIA: Out with what?

JUAN: What's on your mind.

CELIA: I was wondering if you'd like some coffee.

JUAN (*Giving in*): Okay, pour me some. (*Finally looking up at her.*) Celia, What does a person do who just can't take it anymore?

CELIA (*Keeping an even tone after a barely perceptible pause*): He probably shoots himself.

JUAN (*With the same tone*): That would be hard. He doesn't have a gun.

CELIA: Then he slits his wrists.

JUAN: Ugh! Disgusting!

CELIA: And messy.

JUAN: That too.

CELIA: How about an overdose of pills?

JUAN: Too risky. They usually revive you.

CELIA: What more could you ask for? You make the effort, but you don't die... Was it that bad?

JUAN: Was what that bad?

CELIA: That "wonderful young model."

JUAN: I don't know why you call her that "wonderful young model" or use that tone of voice.

CELIA: I was just repeating what you said a minute ago.

JUAN: I'm a real idiot.

CELIA: Can I ask you a personal question?

JUAN (*Suddenly interested in the machine in front of him*): I'd rather have a cup of coffee.

CELIA (*Smiling*): Yes, sir.

(*She exits briefly. After studying the page in front of him, Juan starts writing again. CELIA interrupts him as she puts down the coffee utensils. She looks at him playfully.*)

CELIA: Can I now?

JUAN: Can you what?

CELIA: Can I ask you that personal question?

JUAN: I was doing the interview. Now I'm trying to write the article, if you'll let me. Is that what you wanted to know?

CELIA: What do you mean: "doing" the interview?

JUAN (*Ironically*): More or less what I always mean: ask questions, take notes. You know.

CELIA: For a week straight, without any breaks?

JUAN: That's right.

CELIA: This must be the best article you've ever written.

JUAN: Don't you believe it. I don't even know how to start.

CELIA (*Smiling*): Easy, just start this one like you start the others: "So-and-So lives in a luxurious apartment on such-and-such a street. She opens her door to us cordially, dressed simply in..."

JUAN: Thanks.

CELIA: What for?

JUAN: This isn't the first time you've made me feel like a fool, but today, I really needed it.

CELIA (*Not wanting to take him seriously*): Oh-h-h-h dear! You didn't come home all set to be charming. (*She turns to leave.*) But come to think of it, have you ever tried to charm anyone?

JUAN (*Attempting to match her irony*): Way down deep, I'm a charmer. It's just down pretty deep.

(*CELIA exits, and JUAN crosses out what he has written, dragging on his cigarette in deep thought as he gazes intently at the page in front of him. Meanwhile, the lights go up on the space that will become SUSI's apartment. Standing behind the door, loaded with photographic equipment, is MANNY. As soon as SUSI opens the door, the flashbulbs on MANNY's camera begin to pop. Surprised, SUSI, smiles. MANNY, about twenty-six years old, has a lot of personality. He is aware of his charm and does not hesitate to use it. SUSI, the girl in the billboard and TV ads, is about twenty. Although less beautiful than in the pictures, she is more appealing.*)

MANNY: Hi! I'm Manny Gomez from *Woman Talk* magazine.

SUSI: Yes, I figured.

MANNY: Sorry to have kept you waiting. What happened was...

SUSI (*Interrupting him*): No problem. Come on in.

MANNY: First we have to get a guy out of the elevator.

SUSI: What guy?

MANNY: Gomez. The one who's going to ask all those dumb questions. He's stuck in the elevator.

SUSI: In the elevator?

MANNY: In the elevator.

SUSI: Then how did you get out?

MANNY: I didn't have to. I just got here, so I had to walk up. It looks like he's been in there quite a while.

SUSI: Poor thing! He must have claustrophobia by now.

MANNY (*Laughing*): I wouldn't be surprised. I could hear him kicking the door. He's not yelling yet, but it's probably because he's too embarrassed.

SUSI (*Decisively*): I'll call the super.

MANNY: Don't bother. There's no one down there.

SUSI: Oh, he lives in another building. But I have his telephone number somewhere.

(*SUSI goes for a small address book and looks up the number.*)

MANNY: If he doesn't live here, who did I call from the street?

SUSI: You rang the ground-floor apartment, and it's empty.

MANNY: That's a coincidence.

SUSI: Not really. A lot of these apartments are empty, and in the summer, there's nobody around. (*Referring to JUAN.*) Tell that guy to be patient. We're going to get him out soon.

MANNY (*Putting down his photographic equipment*): I'm off.

SUSI: What floor did he get stuck on?

MANNY: Between this one and the one below. You didn't hear anything?

(MANNY exits. SUSI goes toward the telephone--the same one that JUAN used, if possible--and dials a number. The scene shifts back to JUAN and CELIA. The latter has a coffee pot in her hand and the same playful expression on her face.)

CELIA: About not being able to take it anymore: am I included in that "it," by any chance?

JUAN (*Wearily*): Will you let me work, Celia, please?

CELIA: I just want to know if I'm included or not.

JUAN (*Resigning himself*): In what?

CELIA (*Pouring coffee into JUAN's cup*): In what you said about not being able to take it anymore.

JUAN: When did I say that?

CELIA: Just now, on the telephone.

JUAN: I was talking to Martinez about work. Why would I be talking about you?

CELIA: I don't know. But were you?

JUAN: Was I what?

CELIA: Feeling like you can't take *me* anymore?

JUAN: At four in the morning, you decide to ask esoteric questions?

CELIA (*Beginning to laugh*): I decide *what*, you say?

(SUSI, impatient, hangs up, re-dials and waits.)

JUAN: No, you're not what I can't take anymore.

CELIA: Well, that's consoling... But I'd appreciate something a bit more positive, a certain... How shall I put it?... A certain recognition of my role... my help, at least. (*Still in a joking manner, and as though suddenly remembering something.*) Six years! Really, that's a long time. Do you think we should give some thought to ending it all?

JUAN (*Looking at her steadily and emphasizing the importance of his reply*): Yes, I do.

(At that moment, SUSI, tired of waiting for a response, hangs up and leaves quickly through the apartment door, slamming it behind her. She stops a moment in front of the elevator, straining to hear something. Between CELIA and JUAN, there is a pause. CELIA looks at JUAN without reacting, and JUAN continues to look her in the eye very steadily.)

CELIA: I think you're serious.

JUAN: I *am* serious, Celia.

CELIA (*Attempting to pass it off*): Well, gee... I guess I should have gone back to bed. (*She goes toward the door.*)

JUAN: Wait...

CELIA: Forget it. This has been coming on for some time now, hasn't it? I'd rather you didn't say anything else... But just tell me one thing: what made you come to this decision? Was it the "wonderful young model"? (*JUAN looks at her a few moments as though not knowing what to respond. Finally, he nods affirmatively.*) Congratulations. And good luck with the article. (*JUAN stands up and makes a gesture to stop her.*)

JUAN: Celia...

CELIA: Get back to work.

(CELIA exits. JUAN seems immobilized, as though not knowing what to do. Then, nervously, he turns again to his typewriter, tears out the page, rips it to pieces and tosses it away. He gets up brusquely, just to be doing something and then lights another cigarette. At the stairway landing, MANNY appears.)

MANNY (*To SUSI*): What's new?

SUSI: Nothing. There's no answer. I don't know what to do.

MANNY: I know what we can do: eat.

SUSI (*Pointing toward the elevator*): And what about that poor guy down there?

MANNY: Maybe we can find some way to give him a glass of water. That'll make him feel better while we wait.

SUSI: But the super won't be back till tonight.

MANNY: You got a better idea?

SUSI: No. Want something to drink?

MANNY: Whacha got?

SUSI: Beer, soda, things like that.

MANNY: Anything else?

SUSI: Whisky?

MANNY: Good stuff?

SUSI: Not bad.

MANNY: Okay. I'll have some. And the "sandwiched" too.

SUSI (*Frowning*): I don't know if I have anything to eat.

MANNY: I was making a bad joke about Juan, the poor guy that got "sandwiched" in the elevator. Get it?

SUSI (*Making an effort to laugh at what MANNY has said*): I'll be back in a minute.

(SUSI goes to the door of her apartment and finds it closed. JUAN puts out the cigarette he has just lit and goes toward the door through which CELIA has just exited. He knocks gently and waits.)

JUAN: Celia...

MANNY (*Toward the elevator*): Food is on the way, buddy. Hang in there.

SUSI: Now you did it. You closed the door.

MANNY (*Alarmed*): What?

SUSI: I don't have my keys.

MANNY: Doesn't one of the neighbors have a set?

SUSI: The super does. (*MANNY is about to utter a strong oath when SUSI puts her hand over his mouth.*) Don't say it. (*MANNY knocks on the wall of the elevator.*)

MANNY: Juan...

(JUAN also knocks on the wall as a third character, the middle-aged, serious and intelligent-looking CORONER, crosses the stage. Immersed in some papers in his hand, he knocks on a non-existent third door.)

CORONER: Nurse...

JUAN: Celia...

MANNY: Hey, Juan, did you die down there?

CORONER: Nurse...

JUAN: Celia, don't be silly. Open the door. I have to talk to you...

CORONER (*Speaking toward the audience, as though someone had opened the imaginary door*): Is that man I told you about out there?... Well, have him come in to see me as soon as he gets here. (*He goes over to a corner of the stage, puts on his glasses and carefully examines some papers.)*

JUAN: Celia, please. I need to talk to someone. Listen...

MANNY: If you've died, let us know, so we can leave.

JUAN (*Giving a hostile bang on the door*): And there's one for you too, buddy. (*He returns energetically to the typewriter and puts another sheet of paper into the carriage.*)

MANNY (*To Susi*): He knows you're here.

SUSI: He does?

MANNY: Sure, if he hadn't known, he would have said something a lot stronger... Hey, ya' know, you speak perfect Spanish, no accent at all.

SUSI: Thanks. You do, too.

MANNY: Yeah, but I'm Spanish.

SUSI: So am I.

MANNY: I thought you were from the United States!

SUSI: Well, I'm from Toledo, as in Spain.

MANNY: But all the papers say...

SUSI: The papers say a lot of crazy things...

MANNY (*Laughing*) Hey, just a minute. The press is like a mother to me!

SUSI: Well, now you know: you're a son of a...

MANNY (*Putting his hand over her mouth as she had done to him*): Don't say it!

SUSI: You know what we should do?

MANNY: What?

SUSI (*Pointing to the elevator door*): We should try to get that little wheel back on the track. I think that's the problem.

MANNY (*After glancing at the possibility proposed by SUSI*): I have a better idea.

SUSI: What's that?

MANNY (*Pointing to the elevator*): Let's put him out of his misery. What do you say we cut the cables?

SUSI: Oh, please!

MANNY (*Decisively*): Oh, well, I guess I'd rather die cracking my head open heroically than doing something ridiculous, like I do every day. But this jerk doesn't deserve it. (*He has crawled into a precarious position between the elevator shaft and the wall.*) Now, what was I supposed to do in here?

SUSI: That little wheel...

MANNY: Can I ask you a question?

SUSI: That's what you came for, isn't it?

MANNY: No, that's not my job. I came to take pictures.

SUSI: Well, what did you want to ask me?

MANNY: Why you turned down all those other interviews and then agreed to one with a magazine like ours?

SUSI (*Hesitating a moment, then evading the question*): What do you mean, a magazine "like yours"?

MANNY: I mean it's a lousy publication. But then maybe you never read it.

SUSI: I took this interview, because I liked what your friend said on the telephone.

MANNY: First of all, he's not my friend. But tell me what he said, anyway.

SUSI: Oh, something like: "I'm not interested in hearing what you have to say, and you're not interested in talking to me... But these people at the magazine want me to interview you, and since that's how I make a living, if you're willing, you'll be doing me a huge favor."

MANNY: I'll bet he didn't say that stuff about it being a huge favor.

SUSI: Well, it was something like that.

MANNY: Maybe. But he's a real cynic. So you took the bait, huh?

SUSI: I didn't take any bait. I just told him to come over. Why aren't you two friends?

MANNY: For the same reason that some people don't have red hair or can't carry a tune.

SUSI: And what reason might that be?

MANNY: It's just not in the cards. It's as simple as that.

SUSI: Did you fix the wheel?

MANNY: I broke it.

SUSI: Oh, no!

MANNY (*Jumping to the floor*): I'm going to get some liquid refreshment. You have a place to buy something around here, don't you?

SUSI: On the corner.

MANNY: You see? God is merciful. What do you want me to bring you?

SUSI: Anything, just as long as it's cold.

MANNY: I'll be right back.

(*MANNY exits. At the same time, JUAN pauses in front of his work, wondering how to proceed. SUSI, alone now, sits down on the floor, close to the elevator. The only separation between JUAN and SUSI is the difference in levels.*)

SUSI (*Loudly*): Hey, if you want to talk to somebody, we can talk about anything you want. Or, if you don't want to talk, I'll be quiet, but I'm here, you know? I mean... you're not alone.

(*JUAN turns in the direction of SUSI's voice.*)

JUAN: Hi. You're Susi, aren't you? Susi Roman.

SUSI: Yes.

JUAN: Ah... beautiful.

SUSI: What's beautiful? My name? Actually, it's Asuncion Gomez Roman. Your name is Gomez too, isn't it?

JUAN: Yes.

SUSI: But they don't call you that, do they?

JUAN: No, you're right. People usually call me by my other last name: Villar.

SUSI: Of course.

JUAN: Yes.

SUSI: Your friend went to get something to drink.

JUAN: He's not my friend, remember?

SUSI: You could hear us?

JUAN: I'm hearing you now.

SUSI: Well, I'm talking real loud.

JUAN: Well, don't. There's no need to.

SUSI: Oh, all right. Are you okay?

JUAN: I have good moments and bad.

SUSI: What?

JUAN: I mean, it depends on the time. Summer, for example, is good. I like the sun. How about you? Are you okay?

SUSI: I'm fine. But I was asking about your nerves. How are they holding up?

JUAN: What nerves?

SUSI: Your friend said...

JUAN (*Interrupting her, amused*): He's not my friend.

SUSI: Okay, your enemy.

JUAN: He's not my enemy, either.

SUSI: Well, that guy who means nothing to you and who said you were about to kick the door down.

JUAN: I was kicking the door so someone would know I was in here. Now I'm not doing it anymore.

SUSI: Strange.

JUAN: What's strange?

SUSI: Nothing's changed. You're just as trapped and alone as you were before.

JUAN: So?

SUSI: Nothing. It's just different when you're not alone.

JUAN (*Continuing to make light of the situation*): Right. Especially when that someone is out there rather than in here with me. That could be worse.

SUSI: But don't you feel like you'll never get out of there?

JUAN: What are you trying to do? Cheer me up?

SUSI: Oh, don't pay any attention to me... But it is awful, isn't it?

JUAN: What's awful?

SUSI: That feeling.

JUAN: Have you ever been stuck in an elevator?

SUSI: No. Not in an elevator...

JUAN: Where, then?

SUSI: I don't know exactly.

JUAN: What?

SUSI: I only know that I'm as trapped as you are.

(*JUAN senses what she's getting at and adopts a cynical attitude.*)

JUAN: Oh, sure.

SUSI: What does that mean?

JUAN: I have to warn you about something.

SUSI: About what?

JUAN: The recorder isn't on yet. Even if I had it on, I doubt that at this distance it would pick up what you're saying.

SUSI: I don't know what that has to do with anything.

JUAN: It means that you can save the philosophizing. We'll do the interview later.

SUSI: Some nice person you turned out to be! Maybe that other guy was right about you... that, uh, not-so-good friend of yours. What's his name?

JUAN: The pretty boy? You're gonna laugh.

SUSI: Why would I laugh?

JUAN: Because he has such a common label: Gomez. That's his name.

SUSI: Well, that makes three of us, then. What's his first name?

JUAN: Manuel, but everyone calls him Manny. But I don't like to play the cynic.

SUSI: You don't?

JUAN: No. Because I really *am* one.

SUSI: And how is it working out for you?

JUAN: I'm not setting the world on fire, but I get along. It was my cynicism that got me the interview with you.

SUSI: Wrong. That wasn't what did it.

JUAN: No? What was it, then?

SUSI: Fear.

JUAN: Fear?

SUSI: Fear. I was scared to death. I needed to talk to someone.

JUAN: Okay, tell me about it.

SUSI (*Getting back at him*): I thought you didn't have the recorder on. (*JUAN smiles, starting to like SUSI.*)

JUAN: I have a great memory. Anyway, we're talking off the cuff now, aren't we? What are you afraid of?

SUSI: It's hard to explain.

JUAN: I'm sure...

SUSI (*After a brief pause*): Where do you get... ? (*SUSI suddenly stops, as though listening.*) Wait a minute! I think there's someone in the apartment downstairs... I heard another noise. Maybe whoever's there can give us a hand.

JUAN: A noise? You want to go see?

SUSI: What?

JUAN: You want to check it out?

SUSI (*Unconvinced*): Well...

JUAN: It's probably Gomez.

SUSI: No, it's in the apartment downstairs, inside. I'm going down there. I'll be right back.

(*She leaves, as though acting on impulse. As SUSI disappears, the CORONER stands up to greet someone. MANNY, serious, crestfallen, nervous, crosses the stage to meet him.*)

CORONER: I appreciate your stopping by. I asked you to come in, because I had some questions. The other day, you were very upset, but perhaps today (*Pause.*).

MANNY (*Interrupting him excitedly*): I know what happened is all my fault. I accept the blame, and...

CORONER (*Also interrupting*): No one is accusing you of anything.

MANNY: What does that have to do with anything? What's important is that I feel responsible, and I *am* responsible. And so are you. Haven't you ever thought that... ?

CORONER: Calm down, please. This is not an official visit. My only duty is to take care of the body, to perform an autopsy, and in due time, make my statement to the judge. You don't even have to talk to me if you don't want to.

MANNY: Ask whatever you want.

CORONER: Thank you. You see, as a coroner, I constantly deal with accidents, murders, suicides and physical attacks of all kinds. I am familiar with violence and death. They don't faze me anymore.

MANNY: You're lucky.

CORONER: You think so?

MANNY: I don't know.

CORONER: What I'm trying to tell you is that for me, this isn't just another case. There are circumstances associated with this one that intrigue me. The article by Gomez Villar was especially interesting. I read it several times. It's really... well, mind boggling, don't you think? (*The expression "mind boggling" amuses MANNY.*)

MANNY: Mind boggling? On the contrary: I find it absolutely logical and reasonable; even revealing.

CORONER: It's just that I had never encountered such a negative and hopeless vision of the world we live in as the one in that article. Do you share his point of view?

MANNY: In general, I do, but I don't agree with his conclusions.

CORONER: H-m-m-m. The article is very well written, very well written.

MANNY: That's the least important thing about it.

CORONER: Using what happened to that girl to make his point was brilliant.

MANNY: (*Shocked*): You think that's brilliant?

CORONER: Yes, I do. I'll be frank with you. I don't usually read that kind of publication. I don't know anything about the world that made this girl an idol, but I recall that I felt an aversion toward her as a person. I really didn't like her. If I'd had some contact with her, I probably would have reacted in a hostile way. I wouldn't have known why, and I wouldn't even have stopped to ask myself why. We ponder these cases of conscience only when the situation becomes serious or spectacular, hardly ever in our daily lives. According to Villar, that's how they manipulate us.

MANNY: Don't you think you're exaggerating?

CORONER: No. I don't think so. That's why I found the article so compelling. (*Softening his attitude, Manny is not so hostile now.*) For that reason and because of some really chilling words. The title, for example: "There Is No Place on Earth." There's not the least glimmer of hope in all those pages. Was that really the writer's attitude, or did the case of Susi Roman impress him so deeply?

MANNY: He always talked like that. Susi just convinced him more than ever that he was right, so he decided to make an example of her, just like you said.

CORONER: What kind of relationship did they have?

MANNY (*Evasively*): I don't know what you mean.

CORONER: I mean, to stay in the house with someone for a week to get an interview... Is that how you people usually operate?

MANNY: In the kind of work we do, not really, but...

CORONER (*Interrupting him*): Then, how do you explain... ?

MANNY: I don't know if I can explain it! Why does everything have to be explained, anyway? At the moment, it seemed perfectly logical. No, no, "logical" isn't the word. (*He laughs, because "logical" seems as out of place as "mind boggling."*) Logical! It just seemed the thing to do. We just couldn't leave the girl by herself. Anyway... (*He stops, realizing that he can't explain what happened.*)

CORONER: Go ahead. Anyway... ?

MANNY: We went to her house thinking it would be the same old thing: an interview like all the others. But we found something much more important there. Juan wanted to do a kind of eye-witness report: a "you-are-there" story, like staying with someone in a cave for three months or crossing the ocean in a sailboat with somebody, or...

(*The telephone rings. If possible, it should be the same one that JUAN and SUSI have used before. The CORONER goes over to answer it.*)

CORONER (*To MANNY*): Excuse me a minute. Hello. Yes, speaking... Oh, yes, yes. Just a minute. I'm going to take this call on another line. (*He puts down the telephone.*) It's a call from the lab about the tissue samples. Would you mind waiting a minute?

MANNY: No, go ahead.

CORONER: Thank you.

(*The CORONER exits. After a few seconds, MANNY stands up, walks over to the CORONER's papers and begins to leaf through them. JUAN*

*has continued to write during the exchange between MANNY and the
CORONER. As the latter exits, CELIA, dressed in street clothes, enters
with a folder under her arm. MANNY's expression changes completely
when he sees her. He puts the papers down and smiles. He is the old
MANNY again.)*

CELIA: Hi, there. Is the slave driver in the other room?
MANNY: Are you talking about Juan or the boss?
CELIA: I'm talking about both of them. I'm bringing in the translations so
the boss'll toss me a crumb. (*She goes over to JUAN and kisses him in an
absent-minded, routine way as she peeks over his shoulder to see what
he's writing. JUAN, uncomfortable, tries to keep her from seeing
anything.*) I didn't expect to see you around the office. I have some gum
if you want it.
JUAN: No, thanks. It takes away my appetite.
CELIA: That's good. Then we'll save money. By the way, did you get your
check?
JUAN: Yes.
CELIA: What's that you're writing?
JUAN: Something that is going to catapult me to fame: captions.
CELIA: Important ones?
JUAN: You have no idea! Miss So-and-So makes her debut.

*(MARTINEZ enters. About fifty, nondescript, and full of nervous energy,
he wears garters around his shirt sleeves and on his head the transparent
green visor of the old-time newspaperman. The same actor who plays the
CORONER performs this role as well. CELIA stares at him, amused by
his attire.)*

MARTINEZ (*Speaking toward the audience*): Medina! Get down here right
away about that photo layout! Hi, Celia. (*CELIA makes a gesture of
greeting.*) Come on! What's happened to the feature of the week? It's not
here yet. (*Before leaving, he turns around as though remembering
something.*) Hey, Juan! You've got to get an interview with that girl in
the big cancer stink. Take Julio with you. (*MANNY looks up, interested.*)
That girl in the ad, you know. There's the phone number. (*He drops a
piece of paper on the desk.*) Her name is something or other Roman
(*Pronouncing "Row-man," accenting the first syllable, as in English.*) and
she's a dancer. They want something about her in the next issue.

JUAN: Her name is Román (*Accenting the second syllable, as in Spanish.*) not Roman. And she's not really a dancer. She does a number in a go-go club.

MARTINEZ: Whatever. Just do the interview, and get a bunch of pictures.

JUAN (*Feigning indifference*): Have somebody else do it.

MARTINEZ: What?

JUAN: Send someone else. I've had it with the starlets and the athletes and the singers and all those people who say the same things all the time.

MARTINEZ: Could it be because you always ask the same questions?

JUAN (*Exploding*): I ask the same questions because all you people care about is filling up pages! Let me do an article my own way and you'll see some interesting stuff. I assure you it's out there.

MARTINEZ: Tell that to the guys in the front office. Don't bug me about it. Anyway, all magazines have a special audience and function. (*CELIA and MANNY laugh.*) What's so funny?

JUAN: The function of this one must be to incite the morbid curiosity of a handful of housewives who have nothing better to think about, so that some detergent or canned tomato-sauce company can pay our salaries. All the readers of this rag want to know is who So-and-So is going to bed with. In order to tell them that, I have to talk about So-and-So's "fiance." Just let me do some "man-in-the-street" interviews--talk to your average citizen-- and if people are willing to talk, you'll see some real questions. Assign me an investigative report on banking, or on why there are so many robberies, or why buildings are bombed, or why fewer and fewer students go to college, or so many other things! People should at least know we're talking about this country and not some place on Mars!

MARTINEZ: Look, tell that to the guys in the front office, like I said, okay? If this magazine isn't worthy of your talent, get a job with some publication like *Vogue*. They must be desperate for your services.

CELIA: Gee, your journalistic ideal is *Vogue*?

MANNY (*Attempting to defuse the tension*): Whatever would we do without that illustrious publication, Bwana? Who would insult us morning and night? Who would tell us that what we write is garbage, huh? Who would inspire us to keep on wallowing in the mire? We need them, Bwana!

MARTINEZ: Don't give me all that stuff about what we do here. I've had it with you idealists! It's okay to have your head in the clouds at twenty, but at thirty, it's time for your feet to start touching ground.

JUAN (*Calmer and more resigned now*): And to start kissing up, too, right?

Martinez (*Giving up*): Look, Villar, don't get me started. I have work to do. (*He starts to leave, but JUAN stops him wearily.*)

JUAN: Martinez... We can't talk about advertising, right? Because how would this magazine ever survive without its advertisers?

MARTINEZ: So?

CELIA (*Joking sarcastically*): And since we have no honor, let's at least protect our behinds, huh?

MANNY (*Imitating her tone*): Which means that if we mess with them, they just may get mad or something.

MARTINEZ: But why would you want to write about them anyway? (*To JUAN.*) Do an interview with the girl, and leave the advertisers alone.

JUAN (*With studied patience*): Let's see if I got this straight: I'm going to interview this chick who has never done anything special other than get caught up in a publicity scandal involving the poisoning of three children, a lawsuit against a laboratory, and the closing down of an advertising agency. So, let's see: what do you want me to ask her? About her vacation plans? Or should we talk about her parents, or what?

MARTINEZ: Look. Can I give you some advice? Don't make me any hotter under the collar than I already am. Just do what you're told, and don't make waves. And go interview that girl, for Pete's sake! Who wouldn't jump at the chance? They say she's refused to talk to the press! This is your golden opportunity to prove you're a first-rate journalist! (*He exits.*)

MANNY: That's great, isn't it? In addition to playing the fool, they want us to suffer in the bargain. (*He exits behind MARTINEZ.*) Bye, Celia, my fair beauty. Hey! Bwana! Don't you want to see my pictures?

CELIA: What role is Martinez trying to play, anyway?

JUAN: It's his newspaperman routine. He must have seen some old movie, and it got to him.

CELIA: Aren't we going out to celebrate your getting paid?

JUAN: Just a minute. I have to call that girl.

CELIA (*Unpleasantly surprised*): But didn't you say that... ?

JUAN (*Dialing a number he has on a piece of paper*): She'll probably tell me to get lost, but at least they can't say I didn't try... Hello... Susi Roman?... Oh, good. My name is Juan Gomez Villar, and I work at *Woman Talk*... Yes, yes, I know, and I understand, but... Look, sorry to have bothered you. I'm not really interested in what you have to say, and I'm sure you don't want to talk to me either, but the people here at the magazine want an interview, and since that's how I make a living, if you'll talk to me... What? ... No, no, whenever you say. Soon, if it's all right with you, because they want the article for the next issue.

(*MANNY is about to leave, but he stops to listen, interested.*) Tomorrow? whenever you say.... At five? Fine. Yes, we have your address. Thanks. See you tomorrow. (*He hangs up.*)

MANNY: She said yes?

JUAN: Yes, Pretty Boy.

MANNY: How about fixing it so I can go instead of Julio?

JUAN: Why?

MANNY (*Ponderously*): Haven't you seen her?

JUAN: Who hasn't?

MANNY: Aren't you impressed?

JUAN: Nope, not at all. She's not my type.

MANNY: Well, she sure is mine. I'm a man of simple tastes.

CELIA: Be prepared for a disappointment. Pictures can be very deceptive.

MANNY: Tell me about it! Sometimes I photograph gorgeous chicks who come out looking like real dogs in the pictures. (*To JUAN.*) We can say that Julio had a photo session with a countess. Around here, anyone with that kind of a title is sacred.

JUAN: And what will we tell Julio?

MANNY: We don't have to tell him anything. Let him find out. Anyway, what's it to him? He's too old to give a damn.

JUAN (*Giving in*): Oh, well...

MANNY: Tomorrow at five, where?

JUAN (*Showing him the address on the paper that MARTINEZ gave him*): There's the address. But don't be late, like you usually are.

MANNY: That's my very own mother talking! (*He exits.*)

CELIA: Congratulations.

JUAN: For what?

CELIA: You have just gotten an important interview and mothered an idiot, all in one day. What more could you ask?

JUAN: For you to leave me alone, to start with.

CELIA: Why did you make that call? (*JUAN sighs but does not respond.*) You get all hot and bothered with Martinez, and for what? To bow your head and go like a lamb to the slaughter?

JUAN: Celia, do we always have to go around and around about the same old things?

CELIA: It's just that for a moment, you made me believe. I actually thought you were going to stand up to the magazine, that you were going to tell them to shove it once and for all... But what really gets me is that you could have a much better job, but here you are, just getting more bitter by the day, and for that pittance they call a salary.

JUAN: So that's what's bothering you?

CELIA: Are you surprised?

JUAN: If I quit this job and become an important writer with a big salary, will you be happy?

CELIA (*Hurt*): You can forget the "big salary" part. It's not important.

JUAN: Okay, but without that, would you be happy?

CELIA: What are you getting at?

JUAN: At what you really want. What is it? To live better? Have your friends envy you, because... ?

CELIA: To start with, I'd like to see you more satisfied with your life.

JUAN: Then don't change my job. Change the country I live in.

CELIA: Oh, here we go again!

JUAN: If you don't like what I have to say, don't make me talk.

CELIA: What I'd really like is for you to *do* something. I've had it with all the talk. If this country is so important to you, why don't you *do* something about it yourself?

JUAN: I did! And I ended up in jail!

CELIA: I did it again! I always seem to set you up, don't I? All right, my poor dear martyr, put on your medals. But you're not in jail right now, are you?

JUAN: That's what you say! I feel like I'm still there... Celia, if I had faith in something or in someone, I'd keep on sticking my neck out, just like I did before. I'd keep on handing out pamphlets, writing between the lines, anything. But I can't fabricate faith out of nothing. Don't you get it?

CELIA: Well, it's certainly a comfortable attitude, very convenient.

JUAN (*Understanding her game and smiling*): After a few years of goading my self-esteem, you should know that I don't have any.

CELIA: Well, then, keep on writing captions and interviewing idiots. But don't expect the Nobel Prize.

JUAN: What makes you think everyone wants a prize?

CELIA: It was just a manner of speaking.

JUAN: A very significant one.

(*MARTINEZ enters again as hurriedly as before and leaves a big stack of papers on the desk.*)

MARTINEZ (*He does not stop walking*): Villar, don't be such a stubborn jackass, and call that number. In this business, we have to do lots of things that maybe we'd rather pass up. Life isn't always...

(JUAN begins to chuckle, and CELIA, uncomfortable, looks away.)

JUAN: I already called, Bwana. I did it already. And she said yes. Tomorrow, five o'clock, at her place.
MARTINEZ *(Looking to CELIA for confirmation)*: Really?
JUAN: Really.
MARTINEZ: Then day after tomorrow, I want the interview on my desk so it can make the next issue.
VOICE *(Interrupting from offstage.)*: Hey, Bwana!
MARTINEZ: I'm coming! *(With his customary haste, he exits in the direction of the voice.)* I want pictures! And stop calling me Bwana! It's wearing a little thin. *(He exits.)*

(There is a strained pause between JUAN and CELIA. Then he, in a conciliatory gesture, puts the papers in his desk drawer.)

JUAN: The guy you live with is no hero, Toots, what can I tell you? But let's celebrate anyway.

(CELIA sighs in resignation as she smiles at him.)

CELIA: Just a minute. I have to hand this in. I'll be right back.

(She leaves in the direction of MARTINEZ's exit. At the same time, SUSI returns. Very excited, she approaches the elevator.)

SUSI: Gomez!
JUAN: What's up?
SUSI: It's the guy from downstairs. He's on his way. He's looking for a tool that will get you out of there. *(Very relieved.)* I don't think they recognized me.
JUAN *(Surprised)*: What if they did?
SUSI *(Taking no notice of his question)*: At first, they looked at me a little funny but didn't say anything. I mean, nothing special... They just talked normally... or at least I think so. They didn't seem to recognize me.
JUAN *(Beginning to notice something strange)*: Hey, Susi...

(SUSI interrupts him, as though alarmed.)

SUSI: We're finally going to see each other. What do you think of that?

JUAN (*Joking*): To tell the truth, it bothers me a little.

SUSI (*Forcing herself to follow up with some levity*): Well, really, my face isn't all that tough to take... Yours is?

JUAN: It's not exactly that it's tough to take, Gomez.

SUSI: What kind of face do you have then?

JUAN: A pretty foolish one, probably.

SUSI: No, seriously.

JUAN: I don't know. I don't pay much attention to it. But it's probably a bitter face.

SUSI: And why is that?

JUAN: Because I'm a bitter person.

SUSI: Then maybe you don't have that kind of face at all. Bitter people usually just look sour. So-o-o...

JUAN: What?

SUSI: Do you have a sour puss?

JUAN: Could be.

SUSI: Well, you know something? Cross my heart: I've liked you from the first. (*She waits a minute to see if he says something.*) And what about me? What was your first reaction? (*JUAN laughs.*)

JUAN: I don't know... I'd have to see you first.

SUSI: Gee! You've seen me in plenty of places! I was everywhere!

JUAN: Maybe, but it's not the same.

(*SUSI, liking what he said, smiles and repeats it.*)

SUSI: No. It's not the same. I bet you didn't like me. Tell the truth. Am I right? Did you ever buy any of... that stuff? Did you ever buy it?

JUAN: That perfume of yours? No. Why?

SUSI (*Harshly*): It's not *my* perfume.

JUAN: Well, I meant...

(*The NEIGHBOR enters with a lever in his hand. When she sees him, SUSI scrambles to her feet, as though guilty of something. She interrupts JUAN.*)

SUSI: Here's the neighbor now!

JUAN: Hallelujah!

NEIGHBOR: I'll bet he's happy someone's here. Let's see what we can do. (*To SUSI.*) So? Your husband been down there long?

SUSI: No, and he's not my husband. He's just a friend.

NEIGHBOR: Oh. Well, anyway, let's see if this works... (*He begins to work with the tool he has brought.*) I thought you were mighty young to be married. But since getting married young is "in" these days.... Well, getting married or whatever...

JUAN: The world is going to the dogs...

NEIGHBOR: What's that you say?

SUSI (*Frightened*): Don't pay any attention to him.

(*The NEIGHBOR knows perfectly well who SUSI is and shows it. He wants to tell her but doesn't know how. SUSI is alarmed.*)

NEIGHBOR (*Getting bolder*): Excuse me, but don't I know you from somewhere?

SUSI: ... Maybe.

NEIGHBOR: Could it be from TV?

SUSI: I guess, maybe...

NEIGHBOR: Do you work on TV?

JUAN (*Spoiling the NEIGHBOR's game*): She's the one in the perfume ad.

NEIGHBOR (*As though suddenly remembering*): That's it! You're that girl in the big cancer thing!

SUSI (*Screaming*): No!

(*The NEIGHBOR stops abruptly, and JUAN beats on the wall several times.*)

JUAN: Susi...

SUSI (*Anguished*): I didn't even know what they were going to advertise.

NEIGHBOR: Sure.

SUSI: Don't you believe me?

NEIGHBOR (*Becoming more and more uncomfortable*): Why wouldn't I believe you?

JUAN: Susi...

SUSI (*Sharply*): What?

JUAN: What's the matter?

SUSI: Nothing.

(*The NEIGHBOR makes another attempt at repairing the elevator and tries to restore a normal tone.*)

NEIGHBOR: I think that this door...

SUSI (*Forcing herself to be cordial again*): Well, that little wheel up there is broken.

NEIGHBOR: Oh, boy. Yeah, we'd heard that you were in the neighborhood, but we never figured you'd be right here in the same building with us.

SUSI (*Upset again*): And that bothers you?

NEIGHBOR (*Becoming impatient*): Look, I'm sorry, but...

SUSI: You think I'm stupid? You think I don't know how people look at me? You and your wife. Both of you.

NEIGHBOR: But...

SUSI: What do you think? Does it offend you to have to pass me on the stairs? Or do I scare you, or what?

NEIGHBOR: Listen, I never did anything to you.

SUSI: Oh, no? What do you call looking at me like I have the plague?

NEIGHBOR: Wait a minute, I never...

SUSI: They paid me for those pictures. Tell that to your wife. Go on. Tell her and all her little friends who sent me insulting letters after they rushed right out to buy that junk, simply because of all the brainwashing on TV. Or were you the one who bought it?

JUAN (*Alarmed*): Susi!

SUSI: Oh, sure! I bet it was you! "Please, Miss, I'll have some of that naked babe over there. It isn't the smell that turns me on!" Is that the way it was?

NEIGHBOR: Wait a minute! I came up here to do you a favor, and now you're... Say, are you drunk or something?

JUAN: Hey, listen here!

NEIGHBOR (*Preparing to take the ladder away*): I've heard enough; a lot more than I wanted to. (*To Juan.*) And who the hell are you anyway? Somebody else who goes around selling poison? (*To SUSI.*) Well, truth is, when people around here heard you had moved into the neighborhood, they weren't too happy.

JUAN: Get out of here! Leave her alone!

SUSI: Shut up! What business is it of yours anyway? What do you want? Some exclusive interview? You already have it! This gentlemen isn't in that kind of business, is he?

NEIGHBOR: You're nuts.

JUAN: Get out of here, or you won't recognize your face when I get through with you!

NEIGHBOR: Well! (*To SUSI.*) If you want some good advice, move to another neighborhood. Or better yet, go to another country. Because you have the kind of face that people remember. I'm telling you for your own good.

SUSI: I don't want any of your advice! I don't want any of it, any of it! (*The NEIGHBOR disappears down the stairway as SUSI follows after him.*) Idiots! You're all like a bunch of sheep!

JUAN: Susi!

SUSI: Leave me alone.

JUAN: Susi!

SUSI: Oh, shut up!

(*Not knowing what to do, JUAN pretends to be upset, although he is really quite calm in his isolation.*)

JUAN: Susi! Please, I need you to help me.

SUSI: What's the matter?

JUAN: I'm starting to feel sick.

SUSI: What do you want me to do?

JUAN: I want you to get Gomez. Hurry!

SUSI: Who?

JUAN: The photographer, remember? The third Gomez.

SUSI: I can't.

JUAN: Please, Susi, hurry, get him! He's at the corner...

SUSI: Yes, but...

JUAN: Susi, there's no air in here. I can't breathe...

SUSI: Okay, okay. I'm going.

(*She runs toward the stairway but stops there as though suspicious, pausing a moment to look back toward the elevator. When JUAN thinks that she has gone, he lights a cigarette. SUSI slowly goes back close to JUAN.*)

SUSI: Hey...

JUAN (*Startled*): You still here?

SUSI: I'm okay now. You weren't really feeling sick, were you? You put on that little act for my benefit, didn't you?

JUAN: Why did you get so upset?

SUSI: You think I'm a little flaky.

JUAN: Are you okay now?

SUSI: Those people recognized me the minute I moved into the building, the wife, especially. Every time she saw me, she stared.

JUAN: So what?

SUSI: Now they're going to tell everyone that I live here!

JUAN: Will you please get Manny?

SUSI: No! He'll be back any minute now.

JUAN: Are you afraid to go to the corner alone?

SUSI: Yes. (*SUSI tries to laugh as she dabs at tears.*)

JUAN: What did these people do to you, Susi?

SUSI: They really did a number on me, Gomez.

JUAN (*Quietly*): Well, you seem okay now.

SUSI (*Calmer now and laughing as she remembers something*): From in there, how did you plan to do anything to that guy's face?

JUAN (*Laughing with her*): I have no idea.

JUAN: Well, anyway, real punishment would be letting him keep the face he's got.

JUAN: Is he that ugly?

SUSI: Worse yet. He has the kind of face that you wouldn't look at twice. You'd pass him on the street and never notice.

JUAN (*Amused*): Oh! The famous "man in the street."

SUSI: Is that a common expression?

JUAN: The "man in the street"? Yes, you hear it a lot.

SUSI: Well, I hadn't heard it until recently. The first time was when that guy came to hire me for those darned commercials. "Advertising is seduction, baby! You have to seduce the man in the street. He's the buyer." That's what he told me.

JUAN: Did you understand what he was getting at?

SUSI: It was easy. He was the "man in the street." Ever since then, I've been noticing, and it's true: there is such a thing, or just one model, anyway. They all look alike, have the same way about them. I read somewhere that we're all turning into machines: you press a button and out pops a pack of cigarettes. Press another button, and you get a chain reaction. What's a chain reaction, anyway?

JUAN (*Laughing*): It's when one thing makes something else happen, and then that thing causes something else, and...

SUSI (*Quite surprised*): That's it! I'm a chain reaction.

JUAN: You are?

SUSI: First of all, because of the campaign. When they selected me as the "SHE" girl, they said I was going to be a kind of logo. Do you know what they were talking about?

JUAN: Yes.

SUSI: I don't mean just about me, but in general, in advertising.

JUAN: Yes, I do.
SUSI (*Disappointed*): Oh...

(*Being very careful to make no sound, JUAN turns on the tape recorder and positions the microphone close to SUSI.*)

JUAN: But maybe I didn't understand it as well as I thought...
SUSI: The people in the advertising agency turned in different proposals for the campaign, but the company didn't like any of them. And there were good ones, too. I saw them. But no, they weren't having any. So all of those creator people were in a dither.
JUAN: Creative.
SUSI: What?
JUAN: You mean "creative" people.
SUSI: Whatever... it's ugly any way you say it.
JUAN: What is?
SUSI: What those people do. Anyway, those "creative" people were stumped until one day I came in to model clothes for a show on young fashions. That's when they saw me and decided that instead of making a whole bunch of posters... Is posters the right word?
JUAN (*Smiling*): Posters is the right word.
SUSI: So instead of taking lots of different pictures with different models for posters and billboards, they decided to go with a single image for everything, even the packaging.
JUAN (*Nodding*): A logo.
SUSI: That's right.
JUAN: And did you know what they were planning?
SUSI: Well, sure.
JUAN: H-m-m-m... Tell me something, Susi. When they hired you to pose for those pictures, did you have any idea what was going to happen?
SUSI (*Excited*): You mean, did I know anything about what might happen to those children?
JUAN: Oh, no. You couldn't have known anything about that. I meant what all the publicity was going to do to your life.
SUSI: No. I thought of it as a few days' work. I took the job to earn some money. I didn't even think the agency would call me back for other things. But I know why they did, because I became the "in" model. I was just lucky, I guess... Well, maybe that's not the word. At first, anyway, at the time, it seemed like I was lucky.
JUAN: Did they pay you well?

SUSI: For the ad campaign? No, they paid me next to nothing. And then the laboratory put me under exclusive contract.

JUAN: You mean, the agency did that.

SUSI: No, the lab. They didn't want me to promote anything but their perfume. They said if I did, I would lose my identification with the product. Apparently a movie producer talked to them, or something like that, but I was already under contract to them. It came out in all the papers. Didn't you read about it?

JUAN (*Bored hearing the same old story, he turns off the recorder*): Yes, I guess I did.

SUSI: So the press started talking about me. I don't know why. I was on the cover of all the magazines. "Susi Roman, a rising star," they said, and other things like that. Then they began to say I was foreign, that I was a dancer, that I was involved with this one or that one. (*JUAN yawns and looks at his watch.*) They wanted me everywhere. Oh, people just went crazy over me... Until *that* happened.

JUAN (*Interested again*): Until *what* happened?

SUSI: You know.

JUAN (*Turning on the recorder again*): Tell me about it anyway.

SUSI: About the children?

JUAN: What children?

SUSI: The ones who died. Of cancer. Three of them.

JUAN: Is that what you think, too? It wasn't from cancer. They died from some kind of toxic reaction. I don't know who started that cancer rumor. It's probably because cancer gets so much press. It really makes an impression.

SUSI: Apparently *I* was what really made an impression. And I didn't have anything to do with it. You saw that guy who was just here.

JUAN: No, I can't say as I did see him, as a matter of fact. But I thought you were pretty defensive. You really provoked him.

SUSI: I guess that's some kind of chain reaction, too, huh? Maybe I did kind of provoke him, but did he or didn't he tell me to get out of the neighborhood?

JUAN (*Conceding*): He did.

SUSI: And that's nothing. You have no idea of the letters people have written me or the things they've said to me on the telephone. That's why I moved in the first place. They wouldn't even renew my lease. All for the same reason.

JUAN: Hey, couldn't you be exaggerating all this?

SUSI: You come out of there, and you'll see whether the bump on my head is an exaggeration.

JUAN: The what?

SUSI: The bump on my head, from someone who threw a rock at me.

JUAN: That can't be.

SUSI: Oh, yeah? Well, it is. When I was about to go into my apartment building--the one I used to live in--some kids started calling me names, and since I didn't just shut up and take it, a rock came flying at me out of nowhere. And then they began throwing rocks at my window until I moved away. And you know why I moved?

JUAN: Because they wouldn't renew your lease.

SUSI: No, I still had a month left. I moved because they killed my dog.

JUAN: They did what?

SUSI: They killed my dog. They poisoned him, and they left him in front of my door, just like in the movies. That was the day the papers published the story about the third dead child.

JUAN: But Susi, those children died because of an accident, some mistake in the laboratory. There are no guilty people here. The agency had already launched that massive ad campaign with their product, and they couldn't just stop everything in a day. And anyway, what did you have to do with any of that?

SUSI: The people associate me with the whole thing because my face *is* the product to them. I'm the logo, remember? "We're going to show them this girl until her image is indelibly stamped on their brains." That's what they said, and you see? They succeeded. People really associate me with the product. If they could burn me at the stake right now, like in the Dark Ages, they'd do it in a minute.

JUAN: You know, I can't say that I have a very exalted opinion of the human race, but there are a few good people out there. I'm surprised that...

SUSI: Sure there are. That man who just left is probably one of them. What's really scary is that good people do these awful things. Other people make them do it, you know? They let themselves be led. Someone starts it, and then it just keeps rolling. Haven't you ever noticed what happens when you're waiting for a red light to change?

JUAN (*Smiling*): What happens?

SUSI: You never noticed? It's funny. You're standing there with a group of people all waiting for the light to turn green, but while it's still red, you just take a step forward, and everybody starts to walk. Then they're surprised when all the horns start blowing. In my case, there must have

been someone who saw me in an ad and said: "Let's do that girl in."
And see what happened? A chain reaction.

JUAN: Susi, what you're telling me could make a very interesting story.

SUSI: For me, it *is* already interesting. It's the story of my life. Hey, you're
not interviewing me now, are you?

JUAN: Why do you ask?

SUSI: Because if you are, there's something I want to tell you.

JUAN: What's that?

SUSI: You probably came to ask me if I have a boyfriend, if I wear miniskirts
or if I like French films. But I think there are more important things to
talk about.

JUAN (*Interrupting her with his interest*): Yes, absolutely. Go on.

SUSI: I don't know if I can explain it. Before you came, I knew exactly what
I wanted to say, but I'm just not putting it into words very well.

JUAN: Keep trying.

SUSI: I think something started going wrong a long time ago. Something
very important. I don't know what it was exactly, or when or where it
all started. But I see it in everything. I'm just a small part of it, you
know?

JUAN: Yes, I do.

SUSI: I'm just a tiny sample, not anything that makes news. After all, they
didn't kill me. They just slammed doors in my face and left me without
a job, without friends and with no desire to go on living. The result is
the same as if they had sicked their dogs on me. (*There is a strange
noise, and Juan leaps to his feet in alarm.*) What was that? Juan!

JUAN: I don't know. This thing moved.

SUSI: I'm going for your friend!

JUAN (*Anguished*): No! Wait!

SUSI: But... it can be dangerous.

JUAN: Please don't leave.

SUSI: I have to get help!

JUAN: The elevator could fall any minute!

SUSI: That's why I have to get help!

JUAN: Please, Susi, don't go!

SUSI: I'm here.

JUAN (*Trying to calm himself, he attempts humor*): Good God, if this thing
falls now, won't it be absurd?

SUSI: It's not going to fall. Just don't move, and...

JUAN: That's the kind of death I have coming, I guess: sudden and stupid.

SUSI: Juan...

JUAN I suspected it might be this way... an absurd death after an absurd life. I always thought: death can strike at any minute, and, so what? Just one less person, that's all. But what I hadn't counted on was dying in such a ridiculous way, you know? Susi!

SUSI: Yes, I'm here.

JUAN: Please don't leave.

SUSI: Don't worry. I'm not going anywhere.

JUAN (*Nervous again*): If this thing's going to fall, I wish it would get it over with! I'm sorry.... Please talk to me, will you? Tell me something, anything.

SUSI: Now you understand why I told you to come when you called me?

JUAN: What?

SUSI: I was going through *then* what you're going through *now*: terrible fear and the feeling of being trapped, of having only one way out.

JUAN: What are you saying?

SUSI: That I wanted to tell my story before... so as not to be so alone, you know? So that someone out there would hear me. I wanted to pretend that what I went through would make a difference...

JUAN: Before what?

SUSI: Gomez, what do people do when they can't take it anymore?

JUAN: Are you serious?

SUSI: What do they do?

JUAN: Hey, you weren't really planning... ?

SUSI: I gave it a lot of thought. It may sound strange, but that solution was the only thing that kept me going. I kept saying to myself: "Whenever I want to, I can call a halt to this whole thing."

JUAN: You're talking crazy. You're just upset now...

(*Another noise from the elevator.*)

SUSI: Don't move! ... Well, at least you forgot about the elevator for a few minutes.

JUAN: Yes...

SUSI: Be quiet!

JUAN: What's the matter?

SUSI: I hear noises downstairs. I think they're leaving. I'm not going anywhere, don't worry. I'm just going over to the stairwell to tell them something.

JUAN: Aren't you afraid of those people?

SUSI (*Surprised*): Not anymore.

(*SUSI walks quickly toward the stairwell and exits as CELIA enters, dressed to go out.*)

CELIA: Did you finish it?

JUAN: Yes, just a minute ago.

CELIA: You must be dead tired.

JUAN: Yeah, really tired... but, Celia...

CELIA (*Attempting to avoid a confrontation, she adopts a playful manner*): Oh, please, please, no explanations, no explanations. Explanations horrify me. Just wish me luck. I wish you luck, too, and since our paths will doubtless cross from time to time, we'll keep right on wishing each other the best, don't you think? If you like, I'll take that to the office, and you can go to bed.

JUAN: Thanks.

(*JUAN takes the final page of what he was writing from the typewriter carriage. He places it on top of other papers on the desk and hands the stack to her.*)

CELIA: All this is an article?

JUAN: Yes.

CELIA: Gee! It looks more like a book than an interview... Mind if I read it?

JUAN: No, no. I was going to ask you to, anyway.

CELIA: There's a fresh pot of coffee in the kitchen... in case you want some.

JUAN: Thanks.

(*JUAN exits briefly as CELIA sits down and reads with increasing interest what JUAN has written. JUAN returns with the coffee pot.*)

CELIA: This is really good.

JUAN: You think so?

CELIA: Yes, I do. It's much too good for a tabloid. You could sell it to a better publication.

(*JUAN smiles a little bitterly.*)

JUAN: Finish it.

(CELIA continues reading. SUSI and MANNY appear at the head of the stairs.)

SUSI: Gomez! That noise downstairs was the other Gomez coming up.

JUAN: Whadaya know! I thought you weren't ever coming back.

MANNY: I was having a couple of beers.

JUAN: Oh, isn't that nice? Why didn't you take in a movie, too?

MANNY: A guy in the bar went out to look for the super, so I was waiting for him to come back.

JUAN: And did he ever find him?

MANNY: He's on his way up. Apparently getting you out is no big deal. *(Turning toward SUSI, as though recalling something.)* Hey, by the way: what did you do to that guy, anyway?

JUAN: Be quiet, Susi.

MANNY *(Surprised)*: Why do you say that?

SUSI: What did he tell you?

JUAN: Shut up, Manny. It isn't important what an idiot like that says anyway.

MANNY: What's the matter with him?

SUSI: He's just upset in there. So what did he tell you?

JUAN: Nothing. He was nice, willing to help; sent one of his kids to look for the super, who was somewhere or other playing cards. So the guy invited me to have a couple of beers with him, that's about all.

SUSI: Until you told him who I was.

MANNY: Yeah.

SUSI: And then everything changed.

MANNY: I'll say! He even made me pay for the beers.

SUSI: He didn't say anything special?

MANNY: First you tell me what you did to him.

JUAN: Will you shut up, Manny?

MANNY *(Not understanding)*: Okay. I won't say another word.

SUSI: Why not? Tell me. It could be funny. That guy and I argue all the time. I kid him, you know? Come on: what did he say?

JUAN: Shut up, Manny.

MANNY: What's going on around here?

(The SUPER appears.)

SUPER *(In a foul mood)*: Okay, what's wrong with the elevator?

MANNY: Nothing. It's a wonderful elevator. It just doesn't work.

SUPER: If people would treat the equipment right...

SUSI: This elevator has never worked properly.

SUPER: You're the only one who ever uses it, so...

SUSI: I am *not* the only one who... !

SUPER (*Interrupting her*): Turn down the volume! People can hear you all over the neighborhood. (*MANNY looks at SUSI, amused, but she doesn't notice. The SUPER begins to work on the elevator call button.*) This is easy. All you have to do is press here. But you have to do it nice and easy, treat it right.

MANNY: So you lost the card game, huh?

SUPER: What?

SUSI: I need the keys to my apartment.

SUPER: What keys?

SUSI: Don't you have the spare set?

SUPER: I have the ones the owners gave me, but the building president told me...

SUSI: The owners gave me keys, too, and said that you had an extra set, just in case I ever needed them.

SUPER: What happened to yours? Lose 'em?

SUSI: I locked myself out.

SUPER: I won't *give* them to you, but if you come downstairs, I'll *lend* you my set.

SUSI: You started to tell me what the building president told you...

SUPER: Oh, nothing special. But if you want some good advice, start looking for another apartment. The owners in this building don't like renters. That's what the president told me.

SUSI: The one from the United States?

SUPER: Okay, it's fixed now. I'm going upstairs to check the cables, but I think they're all right.

SUSI: Have you noticed how everyone wants to give me some good advice?

MANNY: Everybody? Who?

SUSI: The "man in the street."

MANNY: In what street?

JUAN: Will you shut up?

MANNY: Take it easy in there, little buddy, take it easy. You're going to be out before you know it.

SUPER (*Offstage*): Come down here if you want your keys! And, you: stay up there a minute and press the button when I give you the word.

MANNY: Whatever you say. (*SUSI exits.*) Boy, he's something else!

(*CELIA puts down the papers she is reading and looks at JUAN, shocked.*)

JUAN: Did you read it all?

(He is extremely calm and distant now, as though his mind were a million miles away. During this conversation, he will demonstrate an eerie serenity and pay more attention to the objects and minute details of his surroundings than to what CELIA has to say. He will put his papers away methodically, close his typewriter case carefully, position his tape recorder precisely, take off his watch and ring, etc.)

CELIA: This didn't really happen, did it?

JUAN: Yes.

CELIA: It can't be.

JUAN: You forgot one of the ways, before. You mentioned shooting, slitting wrists, pills. But gas is really a lot easier. It's even cheaper. She's dead by now.

CELIA: You can't be serious.

JUAN: But I am.

CELIA: I don't understand. Why did she do it?

JUAN: She didn't want to live.

CELIA: But that's not a reason.

JUAN: And that's a strange conclusion.

CELIA *(Standing up and going over to him)*: Juan, you would never help anyone commit suicide.

JUAN: Oh, yes I would. And I did. I helped her close all the windows. When I left, she was in bed, listening to her favorite music and breathing in gas. That was five hours ago.

CELIA *(Decisively)*: Where does she live?

JUAN: Why do you want to know?

CELIA: Look, I don't know what happened during those days, but you weren't yourself when you came in here, and you still aren't. Somebody has to get her out of there before...

JUAN: It's too late now.

CELIA: How could you do such a thing?

JUAN: It was the only way out.

CELIA: Out of what?

JUAN: She was practically dead already. They had almost killed her.

CELIA: Who had?

JUAN *(Smiling because what he is about to say strikes him as simplistic)*: People... The system.

CELIA: Don't talk nonsense! That's a cliche!

JUAN: You really think so?

CELIA: How can you be so calm, knowing that... ?

JUAN: Do you know how many people die every day? Do you know how many die for reasons that ought to be a real wake-up call to us all? But no, we keep on sleeping, eating, telling jokes...

CELIA: It's not the same!

JUAN: Of course it is! She at least took control.

CELIA: Give me her address, or I'm calling the police.

JUAN: I don't think you'll do that, but here it is. (*He takes a piece of paper out of his pocket and hands it to her. CELIA rushes toward the door.*) Celia... In case you decide to call the police, don't forget about my article. I want it published.

(*CELIA looks at him briefly and leaves. At that moment, SUSI rejoins MANNY, who has been waiting for instructions from the SUPER.*)

SUPER (*Offstage*): Hit the button! (*SUSI rushes to push the button.*)

MANNY: Now don't panic when you see him, okay? He can be pretty scary, but he doesn't bite. I mean, not usually, anyway.

(*The different levels between JUAN and SUSI are now equalized. MANNY opens the non-existent elevator door, dramatically humming a catchy presentation tune. SUSI and JUAN, now face to face, look at each other. From the side, MARTINEZ enters excitedly waving some papers.*)

MARTINEZ (*Speaking toward the audience*): Hold everything on the next issue! We gotta pull an article. I don't care which one or who wrote it. We're running Juan Villar's interview: cover story and lead article. And I want all the pictures he was in with the girl. Everything in full color!

JUAN (*Smiling*): Hi, Gomez.

SUSI: Hi, Gomez.

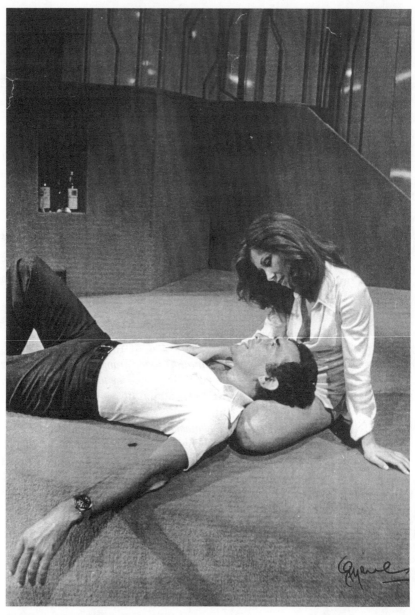

Act Two: Susi (María José Goyanes) and Juan (Fernando Guillén). Photo by Gyenes.

SUSI's apartment. JUAN's head is in SUSI's lap. With one arm over his eyes and a glass within reach, he seems very relaxed. On the record player, Mozart's Concerto No. 21. SUSI looks down at JUAN, affectionately touching his face and smiling as she suddenly remembers something. Taking a sandwich from a plate close by, she playfully offers it to JUAN. When he realizes what she is doing, he takes his arm down and looks at her for a long moment. He smiles and shakes his head to refuse the sandwich.

SUSI: Aren't you hungry? If I were you, I'd eat. This is the last of our food.
JUAN: Manny will be back soon.
SUSI: Today?
JUAN: Yes.
SUSI: How do you know?
JUAN: Because he called a little while ago.

(*SUSI takes his glass and is about to get up. He stops her. They kiss.*)

JUAN: Where are you going?
SUSI (*Standing up*): Your glass is empty.
JUAN: It doesn't matter.
SUSI: Can't I get you something to drink?
JUAN: If you like.
SUSI: But do you want it or not?
JUAN: Well, okay...

(*SUSI pours some whisky into JUAN's glass and stands beside the record player as the music ends.*)

SUSI: Isn't that music beautiful?
JUAN: Yes.

(*The music stops.*)

SUSI: Shall I put it on again?

(*JUAN laughs softly, a bit condescendingly.*)

JUAN: You've already played it twice today.

SUSI: You want to hear something else? (*He shakes his head.*) Why don't you like it?
JUAN: I do like it. But it makes me want to laugh.

(*SUSI returns to JUAN and hands him the glass.*)

SUSI: Want to laugh?
JUAN (*Sitting up*): Yes. Every time I hear it, I think about soap.
SUSI (*Not understanding*): Soap?
JUAN: The one they advertise with that music.
SUSI: This music? Oh, no! This is from a movie: "Elvira Madigan."
JUAN (*Amused*): You see?
SUSI: Do I see what?
JUAN: Susi, this isn't "Elvira Madigan." It's a Mozart Concerto.
SUSI (*Showing him the record label*): Look: "Theme from 'Elvira Madigan.'"

(*JUAN checks for himself.*)

JUAN: What thieves.
SUSI: Who?
JUAN: Well, to tell you the truth, I don't know who's to blame: them or us. But it's certainly a sign of the times. We use classical music to sell soap, beautiful women to sell perfume, and Italian paintings to sell wigs. And we swallow whole everything they dish out. Oh, in small, expertly-packaged doses, of course. One of these days, we'll probably end up selling our own hair to buy a wig. What is this crazy world coming to? (*JUAN seems bitterly amused by his surroundings, including his own words. He speaks ironically, but SUSI takes him seriously, listening adoringly. He realizes it, smiles, and playfully tweaks her nose.*) What are you looking at?
SUSI: I just like to hear you talk.
JUAN: Well, that's a new one for me.
SUSI: Oh, no, I bet that's not so.
JUAN: I don't know of anybody who thinks what I say is important.
SUSI: That's not true. Gomez just sits there with his mouth open when you talk.
JUAN: That's because Gomez is an idiot, and idiots always have their mouths hanging open.
SUSI: I like him!
JUAN: Really? Well, he likes you too.

SUSI: I don't mean that way.

JUAN: What way do you mean?

SUSI: I mean, I like the way he is. He's not dumb, and he's a good person.

JUAN: Yes, I guess you're right.

SUSI: Both of you say you're not friends. Why not?

JUAN: That's one of his little jokes. When I say he's my only friend, he always answers: "Me? I'm no friend of yours!" And he thinks it's funny. He has a weird sense of humor. (*They laugh.*)

SUSI: What about Celia? Doesn't she like to listen to you? (*JUAN looks at her, surprised to hear her mention CELIA. SUSI eventually looks away.*) By the way, you never did call her back, did you?

JUAN: When did I call her?

SUSI: The first day. You called to let her know not to expect you: "Celia, I'm going to be away for a few days. I have some work to do. I'll call you later." But you never did.

JUAN: I haven't had anything to tell her.

SUSI (*Surprised*): Not anything?

JUAN: Not anything.

SUSI (*Disappointed*): Oh... (*There is a pause. In order to be doing something, SUSI suddenly remembers her sandwich and goes back to it. JUAN stands up and playfully takes it away from her.*) Didn't you say you didn't want it?

JUAN: Well, now I do.

(*They kiss again, but soon SUSI draws away gently, unwilling to be distracted.*)

SUSI: I've been doing all the talking, and I'm thinking...

JUAN (*Resigning himself and showing a sudden interest in the sandwich*): What?

SUSI: That I don't know anything about you.

JUAN: I don't know anything about you, either.

SUSI: What do you mean, you don't know anything about me?

JUAN: You've only given me the facts: that you were born twenty-one years ago, that you have no family, because you don't like the one you have; that you don't have any friends, because the ones you had didn't stick by you; that...

SUSI (*Interrupting him*): But I don't know when you were born, or if you have a family, or who your friends are...

JUAN: But none of that's important.

SUSI: It isn't?

(JUAN, taking SUSI by the hand, gets her to sit down beside him.)

JUAN: No. The important things about people aren't the facts. It's who they are as people, what their human possibilities are. Take cities, for example. It's one thing to live in a city and something very different to memorize areas in a guidebook. Have you ever been to Paris?
SUSI: No.
JUAN: So what would you say about Paris?
SUSI: Well, I'd say that it has an Eiffel Tower, the Champs Elysées, a lot of artists... Have you ever been there?
JUAN: Oh, briefly.
SUSI: And what would you say?
JUAN: That I like to go there from time to time.
SUSI: What about London? Ever been there?
JUAN: Only a time or two.
SUSI: Well, I haven't been there even once, but I know about Big Ben, the changing of the guard, what they do in Hyde Park...
JUAN *(Amused)*: What? What do they do in Hyde Park?
SUSI: Oh, people can make speeches about anything they want and sit in the sun in their undershirts. *(JUAN laughs.)* And if I had to say something about Rome, I'd say...
JUAN *(Interrupting her)*: And what about Madrid? Would you say that we have great monuments to Greek gods but no springtime?
SUSI: No. I'd say that's where I met you.

(JUAN is disconcerted for a moment but recovers and kisses her.)

JUAN *(Very tenderly)*: And what else?
SUSI: Well... I'd like to know something about your Madrid, the streets you like, why you like them, the places you go. Then I could tell you about my neighborhood, show you where I was born, the school I went to as a little girl, the park I played in...
JUAN *(Interrupting her)*: And what would you say about me if they asked you?
SUSI *(Immediately entering into the spirit of the game)*: What would they ask me?
JUAN: Let's see, Miss Roman: What is Juan Gomez Villar really like?

SUSI: O-o-o-h-h... that's hard to explain. He's very introverted, you know. He doesn't tell me anything. He doesn't like to talk about himself. And we've known each other a million years. Since the flood, at least, maybe even before.

(JUAN, uncomfortable with the direction of the conversation, draws away from SUSI and gets up on some pretext.)

JUAN: So you were in the Ark, were you, Miss Roman?
SUSI: Oh, no. Juan was in the Ark. In fact, the Ark belonged to him. I was in the water swimming alongside.
JUAN *(Making a "tsk-tsk" sound with his tongue)*: My, my...
SUSI: Well, I wasn't exactly swimming. I was drowning.
JUAN: Uh huh. And did he toss you a rope from up there?
SUSI: No, he didn't have any rope to toss. But he did have two pigs, two hippopotamuses, two ostriches, two of everything.
JUAN: Everything except two ropes.
SUSI: Right.
JUAN: So what did he do, push you under?
SUSI: No. He jumped into the water with me.
JUAN: Oh, good grief!
SUSI: Why do you say that?
JUAN: Because he didn't know how to swim.
SUSI: He learned.
JUAN: He wasn't capable of learning anything, and least of all, how to swim in those waters. *(SUSI goes up to him and puts her arms around his neck.)*
SUSI: Well, he *did* learn. He learned for me.

(JUAN hesitates a few moments, then draws away from SUSI and continues the game as a defense mechanism.)

JUAN: Now, Miss Roman, if you're going to lie, I don't want to hear another word.
SUSI: Well, you tell me how it was, then.

(JUAN smiles and answers without looking at her, with a certain sadness in his voice.)

JUAN: The Ark really wasn't his. He was just another one of the animals. He didn't even know where they were taking him or why.

(SUSI doesn't completely understand what JUAN is saying, but she senses his purpose and reacts instinctively. She knows that she should not speak of anything concrete and that she must continue the game if she is to get what she wants.)

SUSI: But I know why he was there! So that he could save me from the lions.

JUAN (*Laughing*): From what lions?

SUSI: How could you forget? It was awful! And so wonderful afterward. There I was in the arena, terrified, wanting them to open the door so the wild beasts could come out and end things once and for all. The people in the stands were screaming and insulting me. They scared me a lot more than the wild animals. Until you came along, that is. You jumped into the arena and took me away from all those terrible things. You killed the lions and rescued me while all those people kept yelling to sacrifice me.

(When she says "until you came along," JUAN begins to shake his head, slowly, without looking at her, but smiling in an affectionate, ironic way.)

JUAN: I didn't jump into the arena. I was already in there with you. I was just another victim, tied to a post, like you. I couldn't do anything.

SUSI: People can always do something.

JUAN: No.

SUSI: Yes.

JUAN: Okay, go on. What else happened?

SUSI: I don't want to go on. You don't take me seriously. You're always changing the story.

JUAN: You can't imagine how seriously I'm taking you. It's just that you scare me.

SUSI: How do I scare you?

JUAN: It's your imagination. You have a dangerous tendency to embellish things.

SUSI: What's wrong with that?

JUAN: It's not real, Susi. What we don't know *can* hurt us.

SUSI: Since I met you, nothing can hurt me anymore.

JUAN (*Returning quickly to the game*): What if you were persecuted by the Inquisition?

SUSI: Me?

JUAN: It comes after everybody! Everywhere! It pops up when you least expect it!

SUSI: Well, it never bothered me!

JUAN: What do you mean? You told me about it yourself. People thought you were a witch. Three children died, and they blamed you.

SUSI (*Suddenly sad*): It's true... But at first, it was wonderful, you know? People believed in my magical powers and said that I had a special gift. The pilgrims came from miles around just to see me...

JUAN: And your image was on all the village walls.

SUSI: (*Laughing in delight at the analogy*): Yes, that's right.

JUAN (*Reproaching her*): And you let them have their way, and you got involved in that...

SUSI (*Interrupting him*): Because I enjoyed it! I liked being recognized everywhere. I enjoyed having people come up to me. I liked it when they clamored for me and threw flowers at my feet. I enjoyed being loved!

JUAN: They didn't really love you, Susi. One fine day, everything changed, and they began to throw rocks at you.

SUSI (*Sad again*): Yes... How can everything turn upside down so suddenly?

JUAN: Because the very people who adored you began calling you a witch.

SUSI: How could it be so easy for them to believe that?

JUAN: It's absolutely amazing how gullible people are.

SUSI: The only really awful thing in the world is to be rejected or hated. You know when I realized that? One day in the dentist's office... Don't laugh, now. This is the truth. He was drilling my tooth.

JUAN: And he hit a nerve.

SUSI: More than once. But that wasn't the important part. I've always been brave. Anyway, the dentist was real nice and told jokes to distract me. And I pretended to be a very good patient until... You're going to think I'm crazy.

JUAN: Try me.

SUSI: I don't know why, but I began to wonder if this person was really a dentist. What if he was doing this awful thing to me because he hated me, for the sheer pleasure of hurting me? And then I couldn't take it anymore. I pushed him away and jumped out of the chair. Then I began to scream. Poor man! I really scared him...

JUAN: Susi...

SUSI: What?

JUAN: I wish I were the kind of person you want me to be.

SUSI: I don't want you to be any special way.

JUAN (*Smiling*): You believe that I'm capable of saving you from the Inquisition.

SUSI: Yes, because you did.

JUAN: No, I didn't.

SUSI (*Returning to the game, very enthusiastically*): Of course you did! Look, I was like in prison, desperate, not understanding why they ...

JUAN (*Nervous and interrupting very brusquely*): But I wasn't anybody special! (*Softening his tone when he sees her alarm.*) I was just a poor guy who happened to be there... (*Trying to return to the game.*) I was your confessor. But I could only listen. I couldn't do anything for you. (*He sighs wearily and looks away.*) I'm a coward, Gomez. I'm such a coward that I don't even dare speak to you directly about what's on your mind.

SUSI: May I just contribute one cold and miserable fact to this conversation?

JUAN (*Avoiding her gaze*): What's that?

SUSI: I love you.

(*JUAN closes his eyes, deeply moved. He opens them immediately, looks at SUSI and holds her as tight as he can. They kiss again.*)

JUAN (*Pulling away from SUSI*): It has been beautiful, hasn't it?

SUSI: Has been? Are you leaving?

JUAN: Don't you want me to?

SUSI (*Offended*): Well, now I'm not so sure.

JUAN: Think it over.

SUSI: I can't.

JUAN: You don't know if you want me to stay or not?

SUSI: I don't know if you want to stay. Do you?

JUAN (*Smiling*): I don't know either.

SUSI: You see what I mean?

SUSI: But... What's wrong with us, Gomez?

JUAN: Maybe the spell is broken.

SUSI: Why is that?

JUAN: It was probably a trick all along.

SUSI: Sir! Why do you have to see tricks everywhere?

JUAN: Because they're there.

(SUSI, really frightened now, and trying to play down the importance of JUAN's words, speaks to him maternally.)

SUSI: You know what we have to do? Get out of here. We need to clean up, get dressed up, and go out...

JUAN: We can't, Susi.

SUSI: We can't go out?

JUAN: Not together.

SUSI *(Serious again)* Why not?

JUAN *(Drawing her close to him again and speaking to her as though to a small child)*: Because we met on board a magical spaceship in an invented atmosphere outside the real world.

SUSI: And where's the ship taking us?

JUAN: Nowhere. We have to get off.

SUSI: I don't want to get off!

JUAN: Stories have to end at the right time, so they'll always seem beautiful.

SUSI: But...

JUAN *(Pause)*: It had to happen sometime... I'm going to take a shower, get my things, and be off.

SUSI *(Frightened)*: I don't want you to go!

JUAN: I don't want to go either, Susi... But that's the way it is. This is real life.

SUSI: You're going home to Celia?

JUAN *(Shrugging his shoulders to indicate that it is of little consequence)*: Home to Celia...

(SUSI stands looking at the door where JUAN has exited, understanding nothing. Her eyes begin to fill with tears. Offstage, the sound of the shower is heard. SUSI, crying softly, approaches the record player as though in a daze and puts on the Mozart Concerto. The music begins to change, almost imperceptibly at first, but eventually takes on a contemporary sound of violent rhythms. The lights dim around SUSI until only one spotlight illuminates her. She dances to the music as it becomes louder and louder. This spotlight changes into a mixture of psychedelic colors and flashing lights. The small space in which SUSI moves--the same space of the elevator--begins to rise, becoming the nightclub stage on which she now dances in a frenzy. From the side, the publicity AGENT enters. He goes up to her and from his position below tries to communicate through gestures as the music continues.)

AGENT: Hello there! (*SUSI continues dancing without paying any attention to him.*) Hi, honey! Hello! Don't you remember me? (*SUSI does not stop dancing, but she catches sight of him, recognizes him, and waves briefly.*) Will you be long? (*SUSI indicates that she will be finished soon.*) I'll wait for you at the bar. I have good news! (*He sits down before the imaginary bar and gestures to be served. A few seconds later, he begins to drink from one of the glasses used by SUSI or JUAN. The music becomes softer. The flashing lights have dimmed to become low, steady, and atmospheric, as in a night club. SUSI--but not the SUSI as we know her but as she was before the scandal--jumps down from the stage and joins him. She is the garden-variety superficial, fun-loving young woman who rarely has serious thoughts.*)

SUSI (*Breathless*): Hi.

AGENT Hi. What'll you have?

SUSI: I don't know. I'm tired of drinking.

AGENT: How about a whisky? That's a harmless drink. What are you laughing about?

SUSI: I hear that a dozen times a day!

AGENT: Isn't it true?

SUSI: I don't know. It just seems funny.

AGENT: How do you stand it, spending so many hours here?

SUSI: It's no problem. This is how I get my exercise.

AGENT: What?

SUSI: I like it. I can't wait for the intermission to be over to start dancing again. I think that says it all.

AGENT: Why do you do it?

SUSI: You're really asking that question?

AGENT: Yes.

SUSI (*As though the answer were obvious*): Because I enjoy it.

AGENT: Really?

SUSI: Sure.

AGENT: Isn't it tiring?

SUSI: Look. Before I did this, I went door-to-door selling educational records and cookbooks. I've worked in an office, in a department store. I've worked in a gym and been a switchboard operator in a hotel. I can take a lot. So, tell me. Did I get the modeling job?

AGENT: What modeling job?

SUSI: Didn't you say you had good news for me?

AGENT: Yes.

SUSI: I went by the office and tried out as model for a fashion show.

AGENT: Oh, I don't know anything about that.

SUSI (*Disappointed*): Then what's the good news?

AGENT: How would you like to model for some product promotion?

SUSI (*Not daring to believe him*): Who? Me?

AGENT: That's more like it, eh? You'll have to do a couple of screen tests, but, oh, I think it's in the bag. You're just what this company wants. Of course, they'll have to take some nude photographs...

SUSI (*Standing up*): Forget it.

AGENT (*Stopping her*): Come on, let me tell you about it.

SUSI: No, thanks. I already know all about it.

AGENT: Wait a minute. It's not what you think.

SUSI: You're asking me to pose for pictures without my clothes on? In this country?

AGENT: But it won't look like you're really nude. There will be rose petals at the strategic points. You know what I mean?

SUSI: To advertise what?

AGENT: A perfume. It's the first product in a whole new line.

SUSI: Yeah, well, you can get somebody else. If you want, I'll introduce you to Nelly, that blond over there. She'd be great for perfume. She always looks like she just got out of the shower. Besides, she's very tall and very ... everything you want. Come on.

AGENT (*Stopping her again*): But why don't you want to do it? Listen, you wouldn't really be nude. It'd be like...

SUSI (*Interrupting him*): Listen, that's not what bothers me. I'm no prude. It wouldn't faze me to dance stark naked right here. I wouldn't do it, though, because of all those ogling eyes in the crowd. As far as I'm concerned...

AGENT: Well, then?... I'm telling you this is a good deal! Come by the office tomorrow and you'll see it's for real. Don't you understand that this is a great opportunity?

SUSI (*Vacillating*): Really?

AGENT: Imagine! It'd be like starting at the top! It'll make you famous! The opportunity of a lifetime! Understand?

SUSI (*Joking but inclined now to accept*): To advertise perfume, huh?

AGENT: That'll just be the beginning! This will be your springboard to bigger and better things! You're practically in the movies!

SUSI: The movies?

AGENT: That's right! Can't you just see it? Posters, billboards, television commercials, all with your face! With your looks, you'll take the place by storm, you know what I'm saying? This is a real stroke of luck!

SUSI: It is?

Agent: We've had problems with this particular promotion. The company has already rejected a bunch of our proposals. The day you came by the office, they turned down another one, but the head of the group--their group, I mean--said he'd take our logo idea if you'd be the model.

SUSI: They'd take your what?

AGENT: The logo: having just one symbol for everything, you know?

SUSI: Not really, but...

(*The AGENT launches into his spiel like a con artist. The youngest of the the MAN-IN-THE-STREET characters, the AGENT wears sporty, modern clothes, is agile and always appears to be in a hurry.*)

AGENT: It means having just one picture for all the promotion and packaging. Force the image on the public until they think they can't live without the product. In the trade, we call it subliminal advertising. You make people do what you want, and they don't have a clue as to what's going on.

SUSI (*Warming to the idea*): Well...

AGENT (*Continuing his pitch*): This is the way everything works these days: publicity, advertising, promotion. What do you think people do in public relations, business or political campaigns? It's all image. What you see is much more important than what you hear, because you don't have to interpret or even think... (*SUSI nods, attempting to say something.*) They give you everything already thought out. It's a lot more subtle than using words. Advertising is seduction, baby. What you have to do is seduce the buyer, the man in the street. You know what I mean?

SUSI: Yes, I think so...

AGENT: Can I give you some good advice? You gotta open that door when opportunity knocks. You gotta play to win, you gotta...

SUSI: Okay, okay, but spare me all that! What's the deal? I have to jump around somewhere else, right? Just tell me when, where and what time.

AGENT: (*Turning practical now, as though closing a deal*): Then you'll do it.

SUSI: To get all the things you just talked about, I guess I'd jump into shark-infested waters.

Agent: That's what I wanted to hear! In this world, you gotta be where the action is, be where the deals are cut! You understand what I mean?

SUSI: Look, I may not be too bright, but do you really have to ask me if I understand every time you open your mouth? Just tell me when I start.

AGENT: Tomorrow. Be at the office at ten o'clock.

(*SUSI nods in agreement before returning to the platform.*)

SUSI: And thanks for that harmless drink!
AGENT: See ya, babe. Good luck!

(*In a parting gesture, the AGENT raises his arms in a victory sign. From the platform and dancing now, SUSI duplicates his gesture. The AGENT exits. The platform begins a slow descent as the music reverts back to the Mozart Concerto. In the midst of this musical transformation, a note heard in isolation will sound like a machine grinding to a halt. The platform is still now, and SUSI beats on the walls--real and symbolic--that imprison her.*)

SUSI: No, no! Not now! Please God! Oh, how stupid of me! Not now! Please! Isn't anybody in the building? Help! Help! I'm here in the elevator! The elevator! (*Realizing that no one hears her, she collapses and begins to cry.*) Oh, please! Not now! Not now!

(*The Mozart Concerto starts again and continues its normal sound. The platform is completely down, and SUSI will hear the rest of the music with her eyes full of tears. MANNY enters loaded down with packages and a folder full of papers.*)

MANNY: Hello, there, my fair beauty. Here comes jolly old Saint Nick. (*SUSI, startled, dries her tears furtively. MANNY notices and stares at her for a few seconds.*) Where's Gomez?
SUSI: He's taking a shower. (*JUAN enters.*)... He *was* taking a shower.
MANNY (*To JUAN*): Hi. (*Joking.*) You two want me to go out and come back in a little while?
JUAN (*In the same tone*): Better yet, go out and don't come back.
MANNY: Uh huh, but leave the stuff here, right?
JUAN: You got it. And also leave some money, if you have any. We're completely broke.
MANNY: Right away! And since I'm already here, shall I shine your shoes, too, Boss? (*Although JUAN tries to maintain the jocular tone, he continues to watch SUSI worriedly. She turns her back. MANNY finally decides to break the ice.*) You know, every time I leave you two alone, when I come back I get the feeling that about ten years have gone by.

SUSI: Did you really miss us that much?

MANNY: It's not that. It's the changes. You guys are passing through stages at the speed of light... The first day, I was only gone for an hour. When I left, you two didn't even know one another, and when I got back. Gee, if this one hadn't been caged up during that time, I don't know what would have happened.

JUAN: You wouldn't understand. You've never been through anything like this.

MANNY: Let's not get into that, because today I have come to amaze you. I have something here that is going to blow you away.

JUAN: Pipe tobacco.

MANNY: What do you mean, pipe tobacco? This is more like dynamite!

(*MANNY opens a folder full of papers and newspaper clippings.*)

JUAN: What does all this mean?

MANNY: It means that while you two were locked up in here rocking each other blissfully, I've been out working, which is what we came to do in the first place. (*MANNY pauses to ask JUAN a question.*) Will you please tell me what's going on here?

SUSI (*Turning to him suddenly with false animation*): Shall I tell him, Gomez?

MANNY: Out with it.

SUSI: Do you know the story of "Sleeping Beauty"?

MANNY (*A bit surprised*): Yeah, I remember it a little...

SUSI: Did you know that's who I was?

MANNY (*Entering into the game*): What are you saying?

SUSI: Just what you're hearing. And do you know who the brave knight was who came to awaken me with a kiss on the lips?

MANNY: I'm afraid to guess.

SUSI: It's really quite a story, isn't it?

MANNY: A little sentimental for my taste. On the other hand, the one I brought here...

SUSI (*Interrupting him*): Sentimental? It's a love story that's harsh and cruel and unfair.

JUAN (*Softly*): Why do you say that?

SUSI: Because the story doesn't end when the books say it does. (*She is talking to MANNY, who has begun to take some of the clippings out of the folder.*) Do you know what happened when the Princess woke up?

MANNY: Maybe you'd better not tell me that part.

SUSI: She and the knight lived some wonderful days in the castle, without seeing anyone. Nobody bothered them...

MANNY: Thanks...

SUSI: Until one fine day the brave knight announced that he was leaving. He'd lost interest in the princess.

JUAN: Susi, I never said... (*MANNY looks up, curious.*)

SUSI: He was only attracted to her because of some spell. She was just a passing fancy, another adventure.

JUAN: Will you listen to me?

SUSI (*Ironic*): Spare me the facts, will you. Let's just say they aren't important

JUAN: He really wasn't a brave knight at all. He was just a poor...

SUSI (*Interrupting him*): A troubadour!

MANNY: I'm not bringing you two any more whisky.

SUSI: That's what he was! A troubadour! That's why he stayed with her: to write his ballad, because that's how he made his living, and his job was the only thing that mattered to him.

JUAN: Has it ever occurred to you... ?

SUSI: Don't say it! Just don't say anything.

(*There is a silence that MANNY breaks once again.*)

MANNY: Now can this fool, this lowly mortal say something? Here is the Susi Roman file, almost complete.

(*JUAN picks up his glass again and turns away, perturbed. MANNY continues talking to SUSI, who responds without enthusiasm.*)

MANNY: I wasn't able to cut out everything. They used more ink on you than on Rudolph Valentino, but these will do.

SUSI: Do I get a complete set as a souvenir?

MANNY: I have a surprise for you. And for you, too. Are you listening to me, Gomez? (*JUAN gives a nod from his corner without looking at him.*) But first of all, I must confess something. When we came here, we were like two simple little reporters to do a simple little interview for our simple little housewives.

JUAN: They're not so simple.

MANNY: Anyway, what I mean is that I came here to do a job and take pictures of this cute young thing, but when I got here, I was inspired to do some serious work. All these days, I've been digging into the files and talking to people, and I've found a few really curious things. Look at this, for example: the cover picture and story about Susi Roman... "The surprising personality"... "An unusual attraction"... "A new star twinkles on our bleak horizon." All kinds of stuff. Look at this. And this other one is funny too: "Susi Roman is anxious to become a real Spaniard!" What else can she be, for God's sake? And check this about "The rapid rise of a young woman bent on success." And this other one: "Susi Roman, on the road to stardom." To sum it all up, they don't say much of anything: just a lot of insinuation, a lot of color and a lot of pictures. And, hey, here's another gem...

JUAN (*Interrupting him*): What are you getting at?

MANNY: What I'm getting at is that when all those stories were being written, all Susi Roman had done was model for some ad campaign...

JUAN: So?

MANNY: Where I come from, they call that blowing things out of proportion. And you know what kind of money goes into all that hot air? Millions. A heck of a lot more than what cologne brings in, no matter how much of it they sell. And especially considering how little was sold in this case.

SUSI: Well, they couldn't have known that.

MANNY: Apparently they sold so little simply because they produced very little. And they produced very little, because what they were promoting wasn't the perfume.

SUSI: What was it, then: me?

MANNY: No, sweetie. You were just a front. Think back: what else was in the ad, besides your picture?

SUSI: Nothing... Well, there was the slogan: "Yours for the asking."

MANNY: No, there was something else. It was in the movie and TV ads, too. There was something there that you seem to have forgotten.

SUSI: There wasn't anything else.

JUAN: The name of the laboratory.

MANNY: Exactly. And do you know what those famous three children died of?

JUAN: Some kind of toxic reaction.

MANNY: Yes, but not because of the perfume, Susi. That was just another smoke screen.

SUSI: Then, why did they die?

MANNY: Because of a polio vaccine produced by this same laboratory. But more than three children died. There were a lot more.

SUSI: What are you saying?

MANNY: First of all, companies don't advertise vaccines. They have to promote the product in other ways. Second, this company has been enormously successful, much more than average. They can't keep up with the demand. So they get careless and somebody blows it. Third: if a lab makes a mistake producing cologne and three children die, people get upset. They don't panic, though. But if they make a mistake with a vaccine and a lot of children die, what happens? To start with, families quit getting inoculations for their children, and that increases the possibility of illness. And the bad thing for the lab is that they don't make money. So what should they do? Fabricate a story to suit their purposes and then change the decoy--you in this case--since it has already taken the flak. Come over here, Susi. Take a look at this.

(SUSI looks at him in horror and moves to where he is standing.)

SUSI: At what?
MANNY: Your successor. A little tyke, this time, only six months old. Since he can't advertise cologne, he's promoting a lotion. But it's the same thing. Look at the slogan: "How wonderful to feel safe." You see what's going on here?
SUSI: Yes.
MANNY: What a coincidence: The ads with the baby came out in the newspapers first, almost always near an article that talked about the "unfortunate accident that caused the deaths of three innocent little children, etc. etc." Here's a typical one with a wonderful headline: "Shocking photographs turn a young woman into a symbol of shame." How do you like that? Somebody paid for this article. I have it on good authority. What do you think of that?
JUAN: This whole thing reminds me of the Loch Ness Monster.
SUSI: What's that?
JUAN: A monster who comes up in a lake somewhere in Scotland when the press has nothing else to talk about or can't talk about what there is to talk about.
SUSI: Is that what they did with me?
JUAN: That's what they do with everybody, Susi.
SUSI: You say that so calmly.
JUAN: How am I supposed to say it?
SUSI: Don't you realize that you're talking about my life, the only one I have, and that they don't have any right to do this to me? No right at all! *(Turning to MANNY.)* What's the monster's name, the one in that lake?

MANNY: Loch Ness.
SUSI: Well, they're not going to get away with this, Gomez. I'm not someone who just takes things lying down.
MANNY: Of course you're not.
JUAN: How did you find this out?
MANNY: I can't say I did, for sure.
JUAN: So where do we stand?
MANNY: Well, all I did was get the information and come to conclusions, but nobody has actually confirmed my suspicions, you know? To figure out that they're doing a number on you isn't so hard. That's something we more or less have gut feelings about. The problem is that you never really know for certain how they do it or why.
SUSI: I'm not like that. I'm going to find out.
JUAN: How, Susi?
SUSI: By doing whatever it takes. We have to try.
JUAN: Why?
SUSI: Is that a serious question?
MANNY (*To JUAN*): You drunk or what?
JUAN: I'm just asking what we have to gain by knowing.
SUSI: To start with, we won't stand around and let them walk all over us.
MANNY: We can find out why this lab is getting away with murder and who's behind it all.
JUAN: So we could do what?
SUSI: What do you mean? Don't you spend your life talking about how this country has gone to the dogs? So, this is your chance...
MANNY: Exactly! Why don't we start tinkering around to see if we can bring it around!
JUAN: Tinkering wouldn't do any good. What this country needs is radical change, a make-over, a transformation, top to bottom.
SUSI: So let's transform it!
JUAN (*Smiling again*): How in the world could we ever do that, Susi?
SUSI: I don't know how, but...
MANNY (*Interrupting*): I don't know how either. All I know is the news business, and when at last I have a great story... (*Suddenly remembering something.*) Hey, weren't you saying this just the other day? You said that Susi was a good example of how the system uses the individual. You said that what people are really interested in is other people, real people, and that you could do a story on Susi that would bring in all that other stuff. Isn't that what you said? Well, come on. I'm bringing you meat

for the grille--choice cut at that, I think. Or aren't you interested in investigative reporting anymore?

SUSI: Of course he is! Why do you suppose he's here? Show him the notes you've been making all these days. You don't want him to think you've been goofing off, do you? Give them to him. Go on. He can add those notes to his Susi Roman file. I found them last night and read them. I hope you don't mind.

JUAN: Why would I mind?

SUSI: Because researchers don't usually tell their guinea pigs about experiments they're performing on them.

MANNY: What did his notes say?

SUSI: Nothing spectacular. Notes usually aren't very specific. Just a sentence here, ideas to develop there. Isn't that right?

MANNY: Then why are you taking it that way?

SUSI: How should I take it? Don't you realize that he has done with me what everybody else has done? Don't you see how he has used me? Don't you see that he's just like everybody else?

MANNY (*To JUAN*): Come on. What did your notes say?

SUSI (*Going toward the bedroom*): I'll read them to you.

MANNY: Will you tell me what you wrote?

JUAN (*shrugging*): Nothing.

(*SUSI returns with some papers in her hand.*)

SUSI: Listen... Well, not this one. It's from the start. It only has stupid things like my vital statistics: facts, as he says. (*Going through some of the papers.*) But this one, yes. When he wrote it, he'd been here three days, and he was able to spice up his writing. You do that for a good article, you know, to give it a little drama, so the guinea pig will cooperate and tell all. After all, can you think of a more comfortable place to talk than in bed?

JUAN (*Softly and very calmly*): You're mistaken, Susi.

SUSI: I am? (*Reading.*) "It's amazing how easy it is to destroy a human being. Generally it's enough to create a wall of hostility. But even stranger is how easy it is to revive the desire to live. A little of what they call love, and people are ready to go back for more abuse from others who smile and enjoy letting their fists fly. How easy it is to believe in others again and be deceived like a fool." (*JUAN begins to laugh. The nervous tension that has been building in SUSI now explodes, and she rushes at him.*) Don't you dare laugh!

(*MANNY rushes to separate them.*)

MANNY: What the hell's gotten into you two?

SUSI (*Crying again*): That's the only complete sentence he wrote. Everything else is just words, phrases. "Commercially," for example, or "conditioned reflexes." I wonder what he meant by "conditioned reflexes."

JUAN: Will you give me those papers!

SUSI: Sure. They're yours. (*She hands them to JUAN and he tears them up.*) What do you want me to do? Applaud?

JUAN: I want you to listen to me. The sentence that offended you so had nothing to do with you, Susi. I was talking about myself. And as far as the interview is concerned, don't worry. It's not something I can use for an article. What happened to you isn't dramatic enough for the average reader. They've seen children deformed by starvation or destroyed by bombs, and they don't even lose their appetite. The particular problem of just one young woman isn't going to bring in more readers.

MANNY: That's not what you thought the other day.

SUSI: And that's what he still thinks. It's just that they turned down his article. My name isn't news anymore. It's old hat. That's what they told you, didn't they? I'm "old hat." Don't you think that's funny?

MANNY: Who turned down what of yours?

SUSI: Probably a very important publication. In this world, everybody wants to win, didn't you know that? Win at any cost! But he wanted a lot of money for his work, so they turned him down. My manners aren't wonderful, Juan. When you were talking on the phone in the living room, I was listening in from the bedroom. Because I thought you were calling Celia. Isn't that silly? So go on: tell me you weren't using me.

MANNY: What's wrong with what he did? He's a writer, Susi.

SUSI: If your mother were dying, would you take pictures of her to sell to the press?

MANNY: If she was big news, sure.

SUSI: But you wouldn't kill her to get the pictures, would you?

JUAN: She's pretty sharp, Manny, and you always fall into people's traps. Would you mind leaving us alone for a few minutes.

MANNY: You better believe I mind! I have a better suggestion. My car is parked outside. I just filled it up with gas. How about a little fresh air and... ?

(*JUAN resumes his usual cynical, ironic posture.*)

JUAN: Fresh air, you say? It's completely polluted.

MANNY: Well, go out and have a little pollution. Just take my car and...

JUAN: Did you know that the car was the most deadly human invention of all time? Did you know that economic excess is what spurs its production? Did you know... ?

MANNY: So go out for a walk! Do me a favor, will you? Get out of here! Go on. You've been cooped up in here stewing and simmering in your own juices so long that you've just gone off the deep end. There's more to life than talking, talking, talking in here between four walls.

JUAN: That's the way they do scientific experiments, Gomez: in isolation, no contact with the outside world.

MANNY: It's more important to face that outside world, fight for important things, and you...

JUAN (*Exploding and completely serious now*): I wouldn't lift a finger for this shitty country! Who lifted a finger for me when I was arrested? And nobody has moved one since! Can't you see how things are? People are hypocrites. They're interested in you only if you can help *them*. What about all those guys who could have helped get me out of jail? They found it more comfortable to sit around *talking* about freedom over coffee! That's all they do, you know: talk! Look at them, all self-satisfied and preoccupied with their new cars and their fancy electronic gadgets. When three or four of us naive idealists try to do something for everybody, they look in the other direction!

SUSI (*Interrupting him*): Couldn't it be that what's really eating at you is that you weren't rewarded for all your trouble? Isn't it possible that you expected your jail adventure to get you a lot of attention and a better job? Maybe even a new car? Or how about some fancy electronic gadgets? Isn't it just possible that you... ?

JUAN (*His pride completely wounded*): What are you saying?

MANNY (*Conciliatory as always and trying to break the tension*): Hey, come on! Take my killer car, and go out for a little polluted air!

JUAN: You're right.

MANNY: Are you sick? Did you actually say I was right about something?

JUAN: You're right a lot more than I let on. I'm a jerk sometimes. Sorry.

MANNY (*Smiling, he turns to SUSI*): Go on, Susi. Get dressed and...

SUSI: Leave us alone, please...

MANNY: But...

(*MANNY looks at JUAN, as though seeking confirmation.*)

JUAN (*Nodding*): I'll see you tomorrow.

MANNY: You bet you're going to see me. As soon as that sun comes up, I'll be here. I'm leaving you all this stuff. Tomorrow we'll look at it together. Maybe there's nothing there we can use, but I want to look it over anyway, just in case. (*He starts to leave but stops a moment.*) Hey... Gomez. (*Both respond to their names, but he gestures to JUAN.*) You. You're right, we started out being friends, because you were in a position to help me professionally.

JUAN: Manny...

MANNY: But at least we started something, and we're friends, now, aren't we? So this world gave us that, anyway. See you tomorrow.

(*He exits. JUAN sighs, worried.*)

JUAN: I liked it better when he said he was no friend of mine.

SUSI: Why is that?

JUAN: When people feel they have to make a point of saying things, it's usually because there's some doubt.

SUSI: It scary to hear you talk like that! Didn't anything ever work out right for you? Ever?

JUAN: Yes. Once. It was the only time I ever got stuck in an elevator... and when I got out...

(*Before he can finish the sentence, SUSI rushes into his arms.*)

SUSI: Don't you see? You'll *have* to take me with you!

JUAN: But don't you see that I have nowhere to take you? I'd do anything for you, but the only thing I know how to do is my work, and I tried selling it. And I mean sell in the worst sense of the word. You know, that publication I talked to on the telephone represents everything that I hate. Nevertheless, I called and offered myself. You know what happened. They rejected me. They don't consider me a good buy.

SUSI: But just because something isn't...

JUAN: The real failure wasn't the rejection, Gomez. It was having offered myself in the first place.

SUSI: I guess so. And I guess my real failure isn't your rejection but rather my dependence on you. Isn't that right? But thanks anyway.

JUAN: For what?

SUSI: For not being hypocritical... But, what have they done to you, Juan?

JUAN: (*He smiles, remembering her response to the same question.*) They did a real number on me, Gomez.

SUSI: And the funny thing in all this is that you love me. I know you love me.

JUAN: Yes, I do.

SUSI: Then...? (*He stands motionless as he looks as her.*) No. There is nothing we can do. You're going to leave me here alone.

JUAN (*Looking away*): It's the only thing I can do. I'm just not up to starting over.

(*SUSI sobs quietly for a while. Then, as though coming to a decision, she speaks firmly.*)

SUSI: Yes. Yes you can. You didn't let them burn me at the stake.

JUAN: What are you saying?

SUSI: And when you found out that they were going to throw me to the lions, you killed me yourself.

JUAN: Listen, don't be...

SUSI: You didn't want to leave me swimming forever in that space around the empty Ark. That would be awful, much too cruel.

JUAN: Susi...

SUSI: So you helped me out of my misery, because you loved me, and because it was the only thing you could do for me.

JUAN: Will you please stop talking foolishness?

SUSI: Foolishness? When you go out of that door, what will become of me? A week ago, when you found me, I was terrified... desperate, because I had no place to run. I didn't know what to do. But it was less awful then, because I didn't love you; because I wasn't losing you as well. But now, everything's different...

JUAN: Yes, now you're not afraid anymore. You'll fight back and...

SUSI: But you taught me that fighting back doesn't do any good!

JUAN (*Emotional*): No, Susi, I...

SUSI: You have proved to me that nothing does any good; that there is no way out, no hope...

JUAN (*Shrugging his shoulders*): But we have to live. There's no other way.

SUSI: I don't know how to say "there's no other way." And I don't want to learn either!

JUAN: Susi...

SUSI: I don't want to live without you. No, I don't want to.

JUAN: Don't say that. You're young.

SUSI: Is that a reason to live? I don't ever want to be like you! (*JUAN looks at her, shocked by what she has said.*) My love...

JUAN: No... You should never be like me.

SUSI: Juan...

JUAN: You're right, Susi.

SUSI: Then help me. Like you wanted to. Stories should end while they're still beautiful. It's simple. You'll close all the windows, and you'll turn on the gas. They say you don't feel a thing. You'll just leave me asleep, that's all. And then they'll want your interview. I'll be news again. They'll pay attention to you and read what you write. You can tell them all those important things, and some of your readers will understand. Some will even think... What you do will be worthwhile, even though most people have heads made of cement. Even though they don't want to learn anything, there will always be one... And you don't have to be afraid that this is going to be like everything else in your life. You won't have to worry that I'm going to disappoint you, or that after a while, I'll be different, or that I'll leave. You won't have to worry about where I am or who I'm with. You'll stop being afraid of my being so young...

JUAN (*Amazed*): Susi!

SUSI: You think I'm silly, Gomez?

(*JUAN holds her close in a kind of automatic desperation. They kiss. MARTINEZ enters from the side, dressed exactly as at the end of the first act.*)

MARTINEZ (*Speaking toward the audience*): Hold everything on the next issue! We gotta pull an article. I don't care which one or who wrote it. We're running Juan Villar's interview: cover story and lead article. And I want all the pictures he was in with the girl. Everything in full color!

(*He exits at the side. SUSI and JUAN separate.*)

SUSI (*Beginning to get frightened*): But do it right now! Juan! Right now!

(*JUAN begins to close windows as she watches a little apprehensively. Soon, she joins in the activity. She pulls the record player close to her and puts on the Mozart Concerto. Having made his decision now, JUAN waits for her at the bedroom door. They exit together as MANNY enters and begins to go through the papers, just as he was doing in the scene*) *with the CORONER. The latter enters a few seconds later. The music stops as he speaks.*)

CORONER: Sorry. I didn't realize I was going to be so long.
MANNY: No problem. I was rereading this.
CORONER: Oh, yes. The article. When are they publishing it?
MANNY: They're not.
CORONER (*Surprised*): Why not?
MANNY: We're not allowed to say that people don't like the way the country is being run. We have to say everything's just hunky dory.
CORONER: I don't understand. He doesn't attack anybody in particular.
MANNY: No, but he attacks everything in general. Besides, you know that in this country, nobody commits suicide. What we have here are "accidents."
CORONER: Is that the reason the article was censored?
MANNY: It didn't get as far as the government office. It didn't have to. The magazine turned it down... well, the editor, I mean. The rest of us wanted it published.
CORONER: That's strange.
MANNY: What's strange?
CORONER: The very fact that it was turned down shows that he was onto something important. And he was right, too, don't you think?
MANNY: Of course he was right... in all but one thing.
CORONER: What's that?
MANNY: That there's nothing anybody can do.
CORONER: And what do you think we can do?
MANNY: I know we can't give up.
CORONER: I'm glad to hear you say that.

(*MANNY looks at the CORONER ironically.*)

MANNY: Can I ask you a question?
CORONER: Of course.
MANNY: Why did you tell me to come here?
CORONER: Well, you see... The official reason was the inquest. We have to determine if this was a suicide, and if it was, whether anyone else was involved. We need to know if a crime has been committed.
MANNY (*Indignant*): A crime? I'll say a crime has been committed! Just read that. It'll tell you who the guilty parties are! (*Indicating JUAN's article*).

CORONER: I agree with you completely, so calm down. I was explaining my official reason, the pretext, we might say, of why I asked you to come. What I really wanted was to talk to you. I am very interested in what you think.

MANNY (*Surprised*): In what I think?

CORONER: Yes. I belong to a different generation, so I don't understand exactly what you mean by certain words, but I sense that they are not positive. Villar's generation had it rough. Maybe that's why I'm interested in knowing what people like you... or like that girl... think. Can I give you some advice? (*MANNY recognizes the question and smiles wryly.*) Don't let what he says influence you too much. There is always something positive in spite of everything.

MANNY (*Painfully ironic*): Can you be more specific?

CORONER: The very fact that you and I are talking about it. I'd like to know what you expect to do?

(*MANNY decides to put an end to the interview and walks toward the door.*)

MANNY: I'm going out to look for the Loch Ness Monster.

CORONER (*Not understanding*): What?

(*MANNY bids farewell to the CORONER, patting him on the shoulder, as he has already done in the course of the conversation.*)

MANNY: It's a long story. (*He exits.*)

(*For a few seconds, the CORONER stands looking pensively after MANNY. Finally, he goes back to his desk, sits down, puts on his glasses and begins to go through his papers again. In her apartment, SUSI staggers, dizzy and anguished. She opens the windows, breathes deeply and seems to wake up. As soon as she can, she goes to the telephone and dials three numbers.*)

SUSI: Please, Miss. Can you give me the number of a magazine called *Woman Talk*? No, I don't have the address... Not listed? ... Oh, please, please, Miss... It's urgent... All I know is that it's across the street from a movie house. The Princess Theater, I think... Yes, that's the one! If you'll give me the address, I'll find it... Thank you so much.

(She hangs up and rushes toward the bedroom, still unsteady on her feet. She returns immediately, hastily putting on the first clothes she can find before going out into the hall. She goes into the elevator and presses the button. The platform begins to descend but stops suddenly, as before, and, as before, SUSI begins to beat on the walls and cry out.)

SUSI: No! No! Not now! ... Good God, how could I have been so stupid, so stupid? ... Not now! Please help me! Isn't there anyone in the building? The elevator! Please, not now! Not now!

(SUSI curls up on the floor of the elevator and will remain motionless. The CORONER is preparing his report. He looks at his notes and begins to prepare the first few sentences, speaking into a microphone.)

CORONER: Your Honor... ladies and gentlemen. We are here to consider the results of an investigation into a possible suicide. I will go into the circumstances and physical evidence that caused death, but I want to preface my report with some reference to the psychological motives involved here.

(The CORONER switches off the recorder and continues working with his papers at the same time that JUAN enters, exactly as he was at the beginning of the first act. He will duplicate those attitudes, gestures and words. He sits down at the typewriter, puts paper in the carriage, lights a cigarette, etc. The telephone rings. JUAN grabs the phone expectantly.)

JUAN: Yes? *(He sighs, disappointed but resigned, when he recognizes the caller's voice.)* Oh, hello. What's up? Sure, I just got in... With her, with the girl.... *(Speaking louder.)* I said with the girl! Yes, until today, until just now. *(Looking at his watch.)* Well, until half an hour ago, the time it took me to get here... Yes, mostly talking... Talking, I said! Why don't you put the phone on your other ear?

(The CORONER pushes the playback button on the recorder to hear what he has said. His words drown out what JUAN is saying on the telephone.)

TAPE: Your Honor... ladies and gentlemen. We are here to consider the results of an investigation into a possible suicide. I will go into the circumstances and physical evidence that caused death, but I want to circumstances and physical evidence that caused death, but I want to preface my report with some reference to the psychological motives involved here.

(*The CORONER turns on the machine again and continues recording.*)

CORONER: It's no mystery to any of us that suicide in this country is on the rise, and for a reason that affects us all: our inability to cope with stress. We are often unable to adjust to a difficult, often hostile environment that...

(*He turns off the recorder and continues working. Meanwhile, in JUAN's space, CELIA enters, dressed as we saw her at the end of the first act. She holds JUAN's article and stands as she did when she finished reading it in the first act. As the CORONER finishes recording, JUAN, no longer talking on the telephone, stands up. He is in exactly the same spot where he was when CELIA finished reading the article. The appearance of this scene must be identical to the scene of the first act.*)

JUAN: Did you read it all?
CELIA: This didn't really happen, did it?
JUAN: Yes.
CELIA: It can't be.
JUAN: You forgot one of the ways before. You mentioned shooting, slitting wrists, pills, but gas is really a lot easier. It's even cheaper. She's dead by now.
CELIA: You can't be serious.
JUAN: But I am.
CELIA: I don't understand anything. Why did she do it?
JUAN: She didn't want to live.
CELIA: But that's not a reason.
JUAN: That's a strange conclusion.
CELIA (*Standing up and going over to him*): Juan, you would never help anyone commit suicide.
JUAN: Oh, yes I would. And I did. I helped her close all the windows. When I left, she was in bed, listening to her favorite music and breathing in the gas. That was five hours ago.
CELIA (*Decisively*): Where does she live?
JUAN: Why do you want to know?

CELIA: Look. I don't know what's going on with you these days, but you were acting funny when you came in, and you're still not yourself. Somebody has to get her out of there before...

JUAN: It's too late.

CELIA: How could you do such a thing?

JUAN: It was the only way out.

CELIA: Out of what?

JUAN: She was practically dead already. They had killed her.

CELIA: Who had?

JUAN (*Smiling because what he is about to say strikes him as simplistic*): People... the system.

CELIA: Don't talk nonsense! Those are cliches!

JUAN: You really think so?

CELIA: How can you be so calm, knowing that?...

JUAN: How many people do you suppose die every day? Do you know how many die for reasons that ought to be a real wake-up call to us all? But no: we keep right on sleeping, eating, telling jokes...

CELIA: It's not the same!

JUAN: Of course it isn't. She at least took control.

CELIA: Give me her address, or I'm calling the police.

JUAN: I don't think you'll do that, but here's her address. (*He takes a piece of paper out of his pocket and hands it to her. CELIA runs toward the door.*) Celia... In case you decide to call the police, don't forget about my interview. I want it published.

(*CELIA, shocked, looks at him long and hard for a few seconds before she exits. Alone now, JUAN gives a tired sigh, as though finally at peace. He straightens up his desk and looks through his records until he finds the one he wants: Mozart's Concerto No. 21. He smiles and puts the record on the turntable. The music begins, very softly. He leaves the lighted cigarette in the ashtray and walks slowly toward the bedroom. He exits. For the few moments while the CORONER works and SUSI remains motionless on the elevator floor, the music plays. At the stairwell, MANNY appears. He pauses in surprise at the open door of SUSI's apartment. He goes in, calling out to her.*)

MANNY: Susi! ... Susi! ... Juan!

(*He goes into the bedroom but returns immediately and picks up the telephone to dial a number. JUAN's telephone rings, but no one answers.*)

MANNY hangs up, rushes to the door of the apartment, goes out, closes the door behind him, and runs into CELIA, who has just come up the stairs.)

MANNY: What are you doing here?

CELIA (*Excited*): Where is she?

MANNY (*Misunderstanding CELIA's intentions*): Hey, I never expected this of you. It's not like you at all.

CELIA: Let go of me!

MANNY: Listen, go back home. Juan will explain everything when...

CELIA: He's already told me everything! That poor girl tried to commit suicide last night.

MANNY (*In disbelief*): What are you talking about?

CELIA (*Trying to get free of MANNY*): Let me go in there, please!

(MANNY leads her away from the apartment.)

MANNY: Celia, people don't usually commit suicide if they threaten to do it. Where's Juan?

CELIA (*Vacillating*): At home. Sleeping peacefully after writing his poem. That's what he usually does.

MANNY: Listen, Celia... Maybe I'm not the one to tell you this, but... it's serious: they've fallen in love. They love each other...

CELIA: You think I'd be here if it weren't for...

(Hearing them, SUSI sits up.)

SUSI: Who's there?

(MANNY goes over to the elevator.)

MANNY: Susi?

SUSI: Who's up there?

MANNY: It's Manny. I'll get you out of there right away.

SUSI: I've been here since last night. Hurry, please, hurry!

(MANNY and CELIA look at each other. CELIA sighs with relief and smiles, a little embarrassed at the scene she has just made.)

SUSI: Where is Juan?

MANNY: Well... (*He looks at CELIA.*) He'll be here any minute... It's just that...
SUSI: He won't come!
MANNY: Yes he will. He just told me...
SUSI: Did you see him?

(*CELIA makes a move to leave.*)

MANNY: No. But I know he's asleep. He was writing all night, and he was very tired.
SUSI: But have you spoken to him yourself, in person?

(*CELIA pauses.*)

MANNY: Well, no, but...
CELIA: Why?
SUSI: Who's that with you?
MANNY: Nobody. Listen...
SUSI: Who is that?
MANNY: It's Celia. Susi, calm down. I'm going to try to open this. What did that guy say to do?
SUSI: What is she doing here?
MANNY: Nothing. It's just that... (*Giving up.*) I have absolutely no idea.
SUSI: Celia...
CELIA (*Very composed*): I came to tell you that Juan will be back soon. This time, to stay.
SUSI: But, didn't he tell you?... Didn't he really believe that I?...
CELIA (*Interrupting her*): Of course he didn't believe it, not for a minute.
SUSI (*Immensely relieved*): Oh, thank goodness.
CELIA: He told me that you... wanted to frighten him. He'll be here soon. (*To MANNY.*) I'm leaving.
SUSI: Oh, Gomez. Life is wonderful after all!

(*This sentence stops CELIA again, who looks toward the elevator in anguish.*)

MANNY (*Struggling to make the elevator work*): It is, isn't it? Hey, what was that about... ?
SUSI: If you knew what I've been through tonight ! Hours and hours in this cage, kicking and screaming, and crying and calling out to Juan...

MANNY: Will you tell me what the super did the other day?

SUSI: Do you believe if you have enough faith, you can do anything?

MANNY: Anything but fix this damned elevator, sweetheart. But how... ?

SUSI: All we need is someone to fight for. If we have that, we can do anything. I feel strong now, like I could change the world! I'd change it for Juan! And I could even convince him that it's worthwhile, that it's not true that things are hopeless. It's not true that there's only one way out.

CELIA (*Suddenly alarmed*): Is that what he said?

SUSI (*Surprised that she is still present*): Celia?

(*CELIA bends over the elevator opening.*)

CELIA: What was it you were afraid of all night? What?

SUSI: Why? What's the matter?

CELIA (*Pressing*): What were you afraid of?

SUSI: That Juan might do the same thing after writing the article. This piece was very important to him. He said it would be the only decent thing he had ever written in his whole life, the only really honest article he would ever write.

(*MANNY stops what he was doing and comes over to CELIA, alarmed now, too.*)

MANNY (*To CELIA*): What are you thinking?

(*Frightened, she puts her hand over his mouth as she continues to listen to SUSI.*)

SUSI (*Pause*): I was out of my mind last night. I didn't know what I was doing or what I was saying. But as soon as I heard him close the door, I forgot about myself, and I was just afraid for him. It was awful. I suddenly realized that he isn't as strong as I am and that he's tired and can't fight anymore... So I ran out after him, but...

(*MANNY shakes CELIA violently, but she seems glued to the spot as though in a trance, her eyes filling with tears.*)

MANNY: What's the matter?

SUSI: What's the matter, Celia?

(*CELIA recovers and represses a scream.*)

CELIA: Let me go! She's right! Let me go!
MANNY: Didn't you say he was asleep when you left?

(*CELIA shakes her head and dashes down the stairs.*)

SUSI: Manny, what's going on up there?
MANNY (*Rushing after CELIA*): I'll be right back, Susi. I can't stay!
SUSI: Don't leave me here all alone!
MANNY (*Disappearing at the stairwell*): I'll be right back!
SUSI: Wait! Get me out of here!
MANNY (*Offstage*): I can't right now, Susi!

(*SUSI beats on the walls and cries out in desperation.*)

SUSI: Wait!... Wait! ... Juan! (*She sinks to the floor, understanding that her efforts are futile.*) Juan, wait for me, please, wait for me... Juan! Juan! Juan!

(*The lights of the entire stage go down slowly except for a single spotlight on the CORONER.*)

CORONER (*Turning on the microphone and dictating very deliberately from his notes*): Juan Gomez Villar, a thirty-eight-year-old male, was found dead in his apartment on the morning of September 2, 1973...

BLACKOUT

CRITICAL REACTION IN SPAIN

"...The old-timers would say that Ana Diosdado knows all the tricks of the trade: she holds her cards close to the vest and plays the trump at precisely the right moment to produce maximum effect..."

Antonio Valencia
Marca
29 September 1973

"...When *Olvida los tambores* was performed, we said that Ana Diosdado showed none of the flaws characteristic of newcomers. The oft-repeated cliche about completely dominating theatrical technique is, in her case, absolutely obvious."

Alfredo Marqueríe
Pueblo
29 September 1973

"This is a good story, and it's well told.... Ana Diosdado has seen with enormous lucidity some of the major ills of our heartless consumer society and illustrates them through two of its victims: a young girl of minimal culture and sophistication who wants to be famous and popular but has nothing to offer but physical beauty, and a journalist of superior abilities who is trapped by his own skepticism and the belief that the exercise of his considerable talents will change nothing."

Fernando Lázaro Carreter
Royal Spanish Academy of Language
Gaceta Ilustrada
4 November 1973